Le Corbusier and the Architectural Promenade

For Alex

Flora Samuel

Le Corbusier and the Architectural Promenade

Birkhäuser
Basel

Acknowledgements

Like the site of a building, the boundaries of a book are very difficult to delineate. The germ of *Le Corbusier and the Architectural Promenade* has been present in all my past writings on Le Corbusier and in my enjoyment of literature and film, but it was Henriette Mueller-Stahl of Birkhäuser who helped me to evolve the proposal into reality. Tim Benton and Caroline Maniaque gave me support with various funding bids. Paul Richens of the University of Bath, with his typical generosity and style, introduced me to Maureen Thomas of Cambridge University's Moving Image Studio (as it was then) who – together with Ludvig Lohse, Monika Koeck, Richard Koeck, Philip Prager and Terence Wright – provided us – then students and staff of the Bath MArch – with a revelatory introduction to the possibilities of film making. One of these students, Dan Moor, then fed me with further books as he continued his research in this area, as did another Bath student Anthony Bowles who also gave me important inspiration at a critical moment. At the same time Dyfed Griffiths and Martin Gledhill bought me time to write by being, as ever, the most generous and tolerant of teachers.

Anne Samuel was very good company while I recorded case study buildings in Paris. Michel Richard of the Fondation Le Corbusier gave me access to the Maison La Roche whilst it was being renovated and Arnaud Dercelles helped me with the provision of illustrations. Once again Denise Leitao took me around the Maison du Brésil, helping me pick chives from its extraordinary roofscape.

Funding for the use of images came from the British Academy. In Cardiff Stephen Kite allowed me use of his photographs of the Usine Duval which was inaccessible to visitors while I was writing this text. Sam Austin, Steve Coombs and Ed Wainwright worked on the production of the drawings. Marie Gastinel Jones once again helped me with translation and my negotiations with the francophone world. Adam Sharr made extremely useful comments about the manuscript at various stages in its production as did Peter Blundell Jones at the University of Sheffield School of Architecture. It was here that Peter Lathey helped me to gather together illustrations. Indeed all the staff at Sheffield were extremely tolerant and supportive in enabling me to finish this book just at the point at which I was precipitated into Headship of this extraordinarily innovative and exciting school. To all these people I owe my thanks.

It is important here to mention Sarah Menin who worked with me on our first book and who would be outshining us all now if circumstances had been different. And finally, my centre of gravity, my family without which none of this would have been possible.

Sheffield 2010

Table of Contents

0.1 **Unité d'Habitation Marseilles, door from hall at piloti level (1952).**

The "promenade architecturale" is a key term in the language of modern architecture. It appears for the first time in Le Corbusier's description of the Villa Savoye at Poissy (1928) where it supercedes the term "circulation", so often used in his early work.[1] "In this house occurs a veritable promenade architecturale, offering aspects constantly varied, unexpected and sometimes astonishing."[2] Taken at a basic level the promenade refers, of course, to the experience of walking through a building. Taken at a deeper level, like most things Corbusian, it refers to the complex web of ideas that underpins his work, most specifically his belief in architecture as a form of initiation.

Le Corbusier's prime objective was to assist people in the process of *savoir habiter*, knowing how to live.[3] "I know that here I am on the essential theme, the great modern theme: HABITATION."[4] Put simply this meant understanding and fully appreciating what he perceived to be the important things in life.[5]

Knowing how to live is the fundamental question before modern society, everywhere, in the whole world. An ingenuous question and one that could be considered childish. How to live? Do you know reader? Do you know how to live soundly, strongly, gaily, free of the hundred stupidities established by habit, custom and urban disorganization?[6]

The promenade would be designed to resensitise people to their surroundings, leading ultimately to a realignment with nature.[7] "You enter: the architectural spectacle at once offers itself to the eye. You follow an itinerary and the perspectives develop with great variety, developing a play of light on the walls or making pools of shadow," the purpose of all this being to help us "learn at the end of the day to appreciate what is available".[8]

There was nothing arbitrary about the way in which the sequence unfolded. Le Corbusier wrote "in respect of our work, of human labour, of the human world, nothing exists or has the right to exist, that has no explanation".[9] At the Swiss Pavilion (1930–32), for example, the "greatest care was taken over the smallest detail,

1   "Circulation" is particularly prevalent in *Precisions* where a section of a chapter is devoted to the subject. Le Corbusier, *Precisions*, p.128–133.
2   Le Corbusier and Pierre Jeanneret, *Œuvre Complète Volume 2, 1929–1934* (Zurich: Les Editions d'Architecture, 1995), p.24.
3   Le Corbusier, *The Marseilles Block* (London: Harville, 1953), p.34. Originally published as *L'Unité d'habitation de Marseille* (Mulhouse: Editions Le Point, 1950). See also "Eyes that do not see" in Le Corbusier, *Towards a New Architecture* (London: Architectural Press, 1982), p.9. Originally published as *Vers une Architecture* (Paris: Crès, 1923), p.9.
4   Le Corbusier, *When the Cathedrals were White* (New York: Reynal Hitchcock, 1947), p.xviii. Originally published as *Quand les cathédrales étaient blanches* (Paris: Plon, 1937).
5   Le Corbusier, *Towards a New Architecture*, p.23.
6   Le Corbusier, *When the Cathedrals were White*, p.xvii.
7   See Sarah Menin and Flora Samuel, *Nature and Space: Aalto and Le Corbusier* (London: Routledge, 2003) for an exploration of what nature meant to Le Corbusier.
8   Le Corbusier and Pierre Jeanneret, *Œuvre Complète Volume 1, 1910–1929* (Zurich: Les Editions d'Architecture, 1995), p.60. Originally published in 1937. Translation from T. Benton, *The Villas of Le Corbusier 1920–1930* (London: Yale, 1987), p.4.
9   Le Corbusier, *The Decorative Art of Today* (London: Architectural Press, 1987), p.163. Originally published as *L'Art décoratif d'aujourd'hui* (Paris: Editions Crès, 1925), p.165.

visible as well as hidden".[10] In terms of meaning, the Chapel at Ronchamp (1950–54) was, similarly, the result of "meticulous research".[11] As André Wogenscky, his chef d'atelier, wrote of Le Corbusier, "as soon as he draws an architectural form in space, he imparts to it an element of meaning".[12]

I am going to explore the possibility that, like many other aspects of Le Corbusier's architecture, the promenade followed a formula, adjusted slightly each time to fit in with the demands of site and programme, but similar in every case. I will argue that it followed a pattern, a particular series of stages and will show how these were reinforced through the use of detail. In the course of this argument I shall examine the cornucopia of sources that informed Le Corbusier's thinking on the structure of experience, in art, religion, rhetoric, film, literature and elsewhere.

Central to all of this is Le Corbusier's concept of radiance developed in the 1933 book *La Ville Radieuse* which, if examined closely, is more of a theogony than a town planning guide. "Therefore, radiant, therefore ineffable, this total potential with banal materials to make our cities, our homes, our houses and our countrysides, the modern world 'radiant'."[13] A radiant building, object or work of art would influence everything around it as in the case of the Parthenon, which Le Corbusier described as generating "lines spurting, radiating out as if produced by an explosion".[14] Radiant architecture would impose its influence upon the surroundings. It would be connected with other edifices and things, both old and new, built in the same spirit and with the same sensitivity to geometry. Furthermore, architecture could be "made radiant" through the use of the Modulor.[15] Taking influence from day to day observations of the world around him; the measurement of cars, boats, buildings; technology and science; ancient religion and philosophy; art, nature and, of course the body, the aim of the Modulor was to facilitate standardisation and eliminate waste.[16] But it had another more subtle purpose, that of bringing people together in close community with their environment, linked together through the harmonious possibilities of number. More than just a system of proportion, it was fundamental to the creation of what Le Corbusier called ineffable space, "flashes of fundamental truth" that were "an authentic fact of religion".[17]

Within the pages of *Le Poème de l'angle droit*, the book that reflects more closely than any other text the workings of Le Corbusier's inner world, found objects – stones and bones – develop faces (Fig. 0.2). They begin to communicate. They are radiant.[18] Connected with other things and buildings, both old and new, built in the same spirit and with the same sensitivity to geometry, they impose their influence upon their

10   Le Corbusier and Pierre Jeanneret, *Œuvre Complète Volume 2*, p.16.

11   Le Corbusier, *The Chapel at Ronchamp* (London: Architectural Press, 1957), p.6.

12   André Wogenscky, introduction to Le Corbusier, *Le poème de l'angle droit* (Paris: Fondation Le Corbusier, 1989), n. p.

13   Le Corbusier, "Où est-on 26 ans après la Charte d'Athènes," May–June 1962, 18 pp. Typed ms. (unpublished, intended for M.P. Delouvrier's book *Le District de Paris*), p.14, Fondation Le Corbusier (hereafter referred to as FLC) A3 01 365.

14   Le Corbusier, *Modulor 2* (London: Faber, 1955), p.26. Originally published as *Le Modulor II* (Paris: Editions d'Architecture d'Aujourd'hui, 1955).

15   Ibid., p.306.

16   J. Soltan, "Working with Le Corbusier" in H. Allen Brookes (ed.), *The Le Corbusier Archive, Volume XVII*, (New York: Garland, 1983), pp.ix–xxiv (p.xviii). Hereafter referred to as Allen Brooks, *Archive XVII*.

17   Le Corbusier, *Modulor* (London: Faber, 1954). Originally published as *Le Modulor* (Paris: Editions d'Architecture d'Aujourd'hui, 1950), p.220.

18   Le Corbusier, *Modulor 2*, p.306.

0.2 **Drawing of a stone from Le Corbusier,**
Le Poème de l'angle droit **(1955).**

surroundings. "Let me recall to your mind that man seated at his table… The furniture, the walls, the openings to the outside… all speak to him."[19] The building here offers structure to the narrative and acts as a protagonist in its drama.[20]

If a radiant edifice, such as the Parthenon, was for Le Corbusier "spurting" lines out to the horizon,[21] what does this mean for the promenade? Where indeed does it begin and end? Wendy Redfield has illustrated how historians have largely ignored the issue of site in their accounts of Le Corbusier's work[22] while Carol Burns and Andrea Kahn have written convincingly about the need to be critical of the traditional view that the site ends at the limits of the building plot, recognising that boundaries are never fixed and suggesting that it is more accurate to think of site as a network, a territory influenced by the act of designing in a specific place.[23]

The limitations of the site are more clearly defined in Le Corbusier's early work, but are less obvious in the case of a piloti building like the Unité[24] where the reduction of tangible boundaries between inner and outer worlds is likely to have been a conscious decision. Here the promenade creates a public continuum from ground to roof, a quasi exterior route through the building, its progress interrupted by the most minimal of glass doors at ground level (Fig. 0.3). These cause a blurring of interior and exterior space, pulling the exterior route into the house and up to the rooftop garden.

---

19   Le Corbusier, *Talks with Students* (New York: Princeton Architectural Press, 2003), p.54. Originally published as *Entretien avec les étudiants des écoles d'architecture* (Paris: Denoel, 1943).

20   Sergei Eisenstein, Yves-Alain Bois, Michael Glenny, "Montage and Architecture", *Assemblage*, 10 (1989), p.113. "The building itself is allowed to make the film" as Le Corbusier wrote of a documentary that was made about the Unité in Marseilles. Le Corbusier, *Œuvre Complète Volume 5, 1946–1952* (Zurich: Les Editions d'Architecture, 1973). Originally published in 1953. p.10.

21   Le Corbusier, *Modulor 2*, p.26.

22   W. Redfield, "The Suppressed Site: Revealing the influence of site on two purist works" in C. J. Burns and A. Kahn, *Site Matters: Design Concepts, Histories and Strategies* (London: Routledge, 2005), pp.185–222.

23   Ibid.

24   W. Curtis, *Le Corbusier: Ideas and Forms* (Oxford: Phaidon, 1986), p.81. Benton notes that in one of the earlier versions of the scheme a concrete triumphal arch spanned the driveway at lodge level. Benton, *The Villas*, p.181.

There is great potential for literary conceit when writing on a subject such as the promenade. However, as I want to find out whether the promenade can be demystified, the structure of this book is simple. In the first part I identify the techniques used by Le Corbusier to initiate people into the pleasures of *savoir habiter*. These methods are referred to in the second part of the book when they are used as a mechanism to chart the genealogy of the promenade.

Although the architectural promenade is a subject that many authors have touched upon in overviews of Le Corbusier's work there are, at present, no books that concentrate specifically on this subject apart from José Baltanás' *Walking Through Le Corbusier* the text of which is very brief. Colin Rowe's writings on Le Corbusier's use of space and route, particularly his lucid description of the promenade of La Tourette,[25] underpin my work (although Rowe focuses more on visual things than on touch and the other senses) as do William Curtis and Edouard Sekler's study of the Carpenter Centre,[26] Caroline Maniaque's work on the Maisons Jaoul[27] and Tim Benton's writings on the early villas.[28]

In *Towards a New Architecture* Le Corbusier observed that "being moved" by a building or a form "we are able to get beyond the cruder sensations; certain relationships are thus born which work upon our perceptions and put us into a state of satisfaction (in consonance with the laws of the universe which govern us and to which all our acts are subjected)," in which man "can employ fully his gifts of memory, of analysis, of reasoning and of creation".[29] These last few words are really important. Le Corbusier wanted to create settings in which people would be prompted to use their faculties of memory, analysis, reasoning and, ultimately, creation in the appreciation of his architecture, this latter stage forcing them to bring their own experience to the building, creating something entirely new.

As part of my task in disaggregating the experience of the promenade I will need to make statements about its meaning but, since Roland Barthes wrote his extremely influential essay *The Death of the Author* in 1967, it has become problematic to assert one particular interpretation of a text or indeed of a building over another.[30] Le Corbusier recognised that a building's meaning is for each person in some sense individual.[31] He liked to toy with the point of view, leaping from first to third person singular – used to suggest an artificial degree of professional distance – and back again in his own accounts of his work. At the same time he was intensely aware of narrative stance, of the viewpoint of the individual vis à vis the viewpoint of the collective, an awareness that would play an important role in the development of the promenade.

---

25   Colin Rowe, "La Tourette" in *The Mathematics of the Ideal Villa* (Cambridge MA: MIT, 1978), p.185–201.

26   Eduard Sekler and William Curtis, *Le Corbusier at Work* (Cambridge MA: MIT, 1978).

27   Caroline Maniaque, *Le Corbusier and the Maisons Jaoul* (New York: Princeton University Press, 2009).

28   See also Antony Moulis, *Drawing Experience: Le Corbusier's Spiral Museum Projects*, University of Queensland, Brisbane, 2002 [unpublished thesis]. See also Anthony Moulis, "Line/form/movement: circulation diagramming as plan technique", http://espace.library.uq.edu.au/eserv/UQ:3600/moulis.pdf accessed 29 November 2009.

29   Le Corbusier, *Towards a New Architecture*, p.21. See also Le Corbusier and Pierre Jeanneret, *Œuvre Complète Volume 1*, p.11.

30   In Roland Barthes, *Image Music Text* (New York: Hill and Wang, 1977), pp.142–148.

31   Within each individual is a "great and limitless void where one may lodge one's own notion of the sacred – an individual, totally individual notion". Le Corbusier quoted in Jean Petit and Pino Musi, *Ronchamp. Le Corbusier* (Lugano: Fidia Edizioni d'Arte, Association Œuvre de Notre Dame du Haut à Ronchamp, René Bolle Redat, 1997, n. p.).

0.3 **Unité d'Habitation Marseilles, door from hall at piloti level (1952).**

0.4 **Le Corbusier, Sergei Eisenstein (centre) and Andrej Burow in 1928.**

Le Corbusier wanted to make frameworks in which people could live out their own lives whilst dictating very strongly exactly what that framework should be. It is one of those paradoxes that make his work so interesting, so expressive of one of the central conundrums of architectural practice, how do you design buildings that allow others to be themselves? To suggest that he saw himself as a conduit for the implementation of cosmic order would do injustice to the full complexity of his thinking. Disbelieving in "absolute truths" Le Corbusier felt that we should "involve" our "own self in every question".[32] Ultimately therefore this book contains my reading of the promenade and it is important to bear in mind the situated nature of my authorship.[33] I have employed my "gifts of memory, analysis, reasoning and creation" to bring forth my vision of what he made possible, and to encourage others to make their own.[34] As Le Corbusier himself stated, "personal experience is the real test".[35]

René Guilleré, one of Le Corbusier's contemporaries, writes with regard to Jazz, "in our new perspective there are no steps, no promenades. A man enters his environment – the environment is seen through the

---

32   Le Corbusier, *Precisions*, p.32.
33   I tend to focus on the role of nature, women, biography and the meaning of architectural detail in my work.
34   For discussion of point of view in Le Corbusier's work see Deborah Gans, *The Le Corbusier Guide* (New York: Princeton Architectural Press, 2006), p.26.
35   Le Corbusier, *When the Cathedrals were White*, p.65.

man. Both function through each other."[36] Taking my cue from Guiliana Bruno who writes of the way in which architecture can be "read" as it is traversed, I shall use the word reader to refer to a person who enters into the experience of the promenade.[37] This is also the word favoured by the film maker Sergei Eisenstein, much admired by Le Corbusier (Fig. 0.4), whose theory of montage will play a significant role in this account.[38] Le Corbusier stated "architecture and film are the only two arts of our time" before going on to note that "in my own work I seem to think as Eisenstein does in his films".[39] Bruno describes his thinking as "pivotal in an attempt to trace the theoretical interplay of film, architecture, and travel practices" so it would seem to be of relevance to this discussion.[40]

It is no accident that the promenade is a term usually applied to the experience of exterior space, the act of seeing and being seen on the famous seafront Promenade des Anglais in Nice for example. In his early, not yet fully formulated work, Le Corbusier's audience is "the spectator" and, ultimately, "the human eye", completely disembodied, floating around the building at a specified height. The eye, for Le Corbusier, is restless and challenging. It "can reach a considerable distance and, like a clear lens, sees everything even beyond what was intended or wished".[41] One of the major challenges of this book is to try to articulate what happens at the crossing of the axes when the lens changes focus and the retina adjusts to sources of light beyond itself.

Whether hovering at the top of a Unité block (Fig. 0.5) or built at vast scale in *papier maché*, as in the scheme for the Ideal Home Exhibition in London (Fig. 0.6) the eye is that of a child's princess drawing, heavily lashed and feminine. In my book *Le Corbusier Architect and Feminist* I drew attention to the way in which Le Corbusier addressed his architecture to a female audience, believing women to have the most to gain from this vision of society. It is tempting therefore to suggest that the reader of his buildings is female.[42] However, in later work the girlish eye is displaced by the more universal Modulor man in the drawings, who now becomes the diapason of all Le Corbusier's efforts (Fig. 0.7), sometimes in the company of woman (Fig. 0.8).

In creating the seven volumes of his *Œuvre Complète* Le Corbusier himself provides a series of possible readings of his work. Several commentators have noted that the drawings included in its "mythopoetic pages"[43] do not represent the building as built.[44] A serious difficulty in preparing the drawings for this book has been the unreliability of the *Œuvre Complète* plans which have spawned multiple inaccurate versions in

---

36 René Guilleré quoted in "The Synchronisation of the Senses" in Sergei Eisenstein, *The Film Sense* (London: Faber and Faber, 1977), p.81. First published in 1943.

37 Bruno, G., *Atlas of Emotion: Journeys in Art, Architecture and Film* (New York: Verso, 2007), p.58.

38 Sergei Eisenstein, "Montage of Attractions" in *The Film Sense*, pp.181–183 (181). See François Penz, "Architecture and the Screen From Photography to Synthetic Imaging" in M. Thomas and F. Penz, *Architectures of Illusion: From Motion Pictures to Navigable Interactive Environments* (Bristol: Intellect, 2003), p.146 for a discussion of the close links between modernist architecture and film.

39 This interview is cited in Jean-Louis Cohen, *Le Corbusier and the Mystique of the USSR*, trans. Kenneth Hylton (Princeton: Princeton University Press, 1992), p.49.

40 Bruno, G., *Atlas of Emotion*, p.57.

41 Le Corbusier, *Towards a New Architecture*, p.175.

42 "In my drawings and paintings I have always shown only women, or pictures, symbols and genealogies of women (Le Corbusier)". Le Corbusier quoted in H. Weber (ed.), *Le Corbusier the Artist* (Zurich: Editions Heidi Weber, 1988), n.p.

43 Sekler and Curtis, *Le Corbusier at Work*, p.2.

44 Ibid.

The Radiant City
Sun
Space
Green

0.5 **Eye in sketch by Le Corbusier from** *Poésie sur Alger* **(1950).**

0.6 **Ideal Home Exhibition in London (1938) from the** *Œuvre Complète.*

0.7 **Modulor Man, Unité d'Habitation, Marseilles (1952).**

various surveys of architecture. The plans in the *Œuvre Complète* tell us little about the real experience of Corbusian domestic space. The absence of dotted lines to indicate the extent of overhead protrusions causes a denial of the depth and variety of the thresholds experienced at ground level. It is however possible that for Le Corbusier the drawings in the *Œuvre Complète* were less compromised, more real, than the imperfect version as built.[45] Conceived as a lesson in architecture and as propaganda for his architectural vision, these volumes contain multiple hidden agendas. Much care was taken with their contents, a close inspection of which can reveal much to an inquisitive reader.[46] It is for this reason that, in the second part of this book, I juxtapose photographs of buildings as they are today with their idealised representation in the *Œuvre Complète.*

Notable here is the minimal impact of the promenade on the curatorship of the *Œuvre Complète.* An examination of the sequences of photos in vol. 1 reveals alternative preoccupations. The photos of the Petite Villa au Bord de Lac Leman, 1925, for example, all seem to focus on the presence of mountains above, through and beyond the building.[47] However the letter that Le Corbusier and Pierre Jeanneret wrote to Mme Meyer describing their first proposal for her house is written exactly in the form of a promenade beginning at the entrance and described in terms of light, view and magnitude of space, culminating in a landscape worthy of "Robinson" (Fig. 0.9). A similar format is adopted for the description of the second project. Despite this the

45   Josep Quetglas, *Le Corbusier, Pierre Jeanneret: Villa Savoye* (Madrid: Rueda, 2004), p.67.
46   Flora Samuel, "Le Corbusier, Women, Nature and Culture", *Issues in Art and Architecture 5*, 2 (1998), pp.4–20.
47   Le Corbusier and Pierre Jeanneret, *Œuvre Complète Volume 1*, p.89.

0.8 **Modulor man and woman at the base of the Unité, Firminy (1959).**

ordering of photos of the Maison Cook (1926) seems to follow very different rules.[48] While the hand drawn illustrations of the Maison Guiette (also of 1926) are once again presented in a strict promenade sequence from ground to roof. So it seems that when Le Corbusier had complete autonomy over his images and their sequencing, as he did when he drew them himself, the ordering reflects his preoccupation with this subject.[49]

The axonometric projection is often used by Le Corbusier to define the elements of a route. As Yves-Alain Bois points out, "there is no central point in axonometry; it is entirely based on the notion of permutability, of infinite transformations".[50] In Le Corbusier's early sketches arrows are used to indicate designated routes within his buildings (Fig. 0.10). Although he stopped using arrows, he never stopped imagining himself into the spaces of his plans. Design drawings often reveal traces of fine lines drawn repeatedly as Le Corbusier's pencil point went round and round the plan acting out the motions of daily life.[51] These, coupled with the countless rough perspective sketches that exist of individual events en route within his buildings, indicate the full extent of his preoccupation with lived space.

48   Ibid., p.130.
49   Ibid., p.138.
50   Yves-Alain Bois, in Eisenstein, Bois and Glenny, "Montage and Architecture", p.114.
51   See for example FLC 29310 in Allen Brookes, *Archive XVII*, p.462.

0.9 **Letter to Madame Meyer (1925) from the *Œuvre Complète*.**

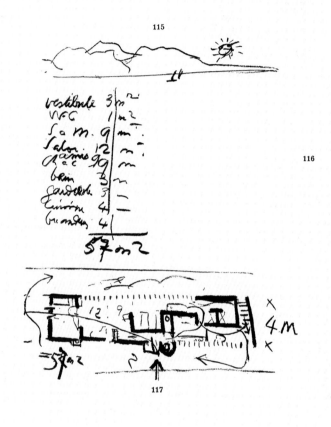

0.10 **"Le Plan de la maison moderne", *Precisions*, p.129.**

"Unity in detail, tumult in the ensemble"[52] was Le Corbusier's stated objective. Although many different individuals helped to translate his ideas into built form, uniformity in detail of his buildings was maintained partly because of the skill and dedication of his employees; partly because of the degree of his involvement in all aspects of design (despite long periods of absence and apparently spending only three hours a day in his office when he was in Paris); partly through the use of a limited family of forms (often derived from his paintings); partly through the – more orthodox, but rare – use of schedules of standard details;[53] partly because of the *Œuvre Complète* – Jerzy Soltan recalled that Le Corbusier frequently told his employees

---

52 Le Corbusier and Pierre Jeanneret, *Œuvre Complète Volume 1*, p.132.
53 See for example FLC 17396 in Allen Brookes, *Archive XXIX*, p.392 or FLC 5461 in Allen Brookes, *Archive XXV*, p.405.

21

to "Go and check this in the Girsberger", meaning the *Œuvre Complète*, in this way "assuring his work's continuity, saving time and money";[54] and partly through the use of his system of proportion, the Modulor, used to "prevent [elements] from being in arbitrary relation to one another, to make them adjust precisely to one another, to bring them together in one single family."[55]

The vital role of his cousin Pierre Jeanneret should be emphasised in all this. Whilst, as a matter of principle, I try to emphasise that architecture is the product of team work rather than that of the individual genius Le Corbusier's production of words swamps Jeanneret's reticence and makes it difficult to ascertain where the authorship of one begins and the other ends.[56] Were Le Corbusier's collaborators readers or writers, directors or producers? Le Corbusier's name becomes an icon, a brand that takes over his own personal identity Charles Edouard Jeanneret and encompasses the work of the entire practice. It is one thing to design a pioneering building, another thing to get it made. Le Corbusier's work is only as good as that of the people that worked for him, whether on site or in his atelier, something of which he was fully aware.

As I take seriously Jeremy Till's call for a recognition of the contingent nature of architectural practice, I am concerned that this book should not just comprise a litany of succulent details or that it should focus too much on formal issues or aesthetics.[57] This and its predecessor were written because I wanted to show that, instead of being a genius with hidden powers inaccessible to the rest of us mere mortals, Le Corbusier was a human being who, with the help and ideas of the people around him, used particular techniques and families of detail to achieve his remarkable architecture. Further that, unlike many of his contemporaries, he recognised the thorny complexity of creating a contingent architecture, an architecture celebratory of the life within it.[58]

Architecture is a precarious business. Certainly in the United Kingdom architects seem to have difficulty in explaining to the general public the validity of what they do. There is much discussion of the issue of quality, of what constitutes good architecture which seems to be something left deliberately hazy, although there have been some valiant attempts to rectify this situation.[59] Le Corbusier's buildings are the result of skilful manipulation of detail and space planning, which, I believe, can be described, learnt from and conceivably given value.

I feel strongly about this at a time when basic skills of design are being eroded by the nascent world of digitally generated images which, despite appearances to the contrary, often avoid real investigation of the tectonic pleasures of route and space. I am not necessarily arguing for a luddite pre-digital world, but for a melding of this territory with that of film theory and game space in which narrative and meaning can be

---

54   Soltan, "Working with Le Corbusier" in Allen Brookes, *Archive XVII*, p.xxiii.

55   André Wogenscky, "The Unité d'Habitation at Marseille" in Allen Brookes, *Archive XVI*, p. xvii.

56   Maristella Casciato's research on Jeanneret should do much to redress this balance.

57   Jeremy Till, *Architecture Depends* (Cambridge MA: MIT, 2009), p.176.

58   Whether he would have liked it or not, his buildings lend themselves to adaptation as has been seen at Pessac. See Philippe Boudon's discussion of changes made by the inhabitants of Le Corbusier's Pessac scheme. P. Boudon, *Lived-in Architecture* (Cambridge MA: MIT, 1972), p.1.

59   See Juliet Odgers and Flora Samuel, "Design Quality Indicators" in Allison Dutoit, Juliet Odgers and Adam Sharr, *Quality Out of Control* (London: Routledge, 2010), p.xvii.

0.11 **Mannequin in the window of Villa Cook from the *Œuvre Complète*.**

somehow reasserted.[60] This is architectural history conceived to inform practice and debate. It is not, I very much hope, an end in itself.

The delights of architectural detail as art – spatial games and hidden meanings – are the territory of the rarefied few who enter into the club of architecture, but I believe, as did Le Corbusier, that buildings can be read in a variety of different ways depending upon who is doing the reading. We should try to create architecture that allows the readings of others into the fold. Whilst he might have used all sorts of abstract, didactic, rigid and formal techniques in the evolution of his ideas, techniques that largely deny the fluidity of human existence, Le Corbusier did at least try, if not always successfully, to address how others might experience his buildings, and to reinforce the message that his buildings were conceived of as incomplete without people.[61] (Fig. 0.11)

---

60   See for example the work of Maureen Thomas and the Cambridge University Moving Image Studio.
61   Le Corbusier and Pierre Jeanneret, *Œuvre Complète Volume 1*, pp.134–135.

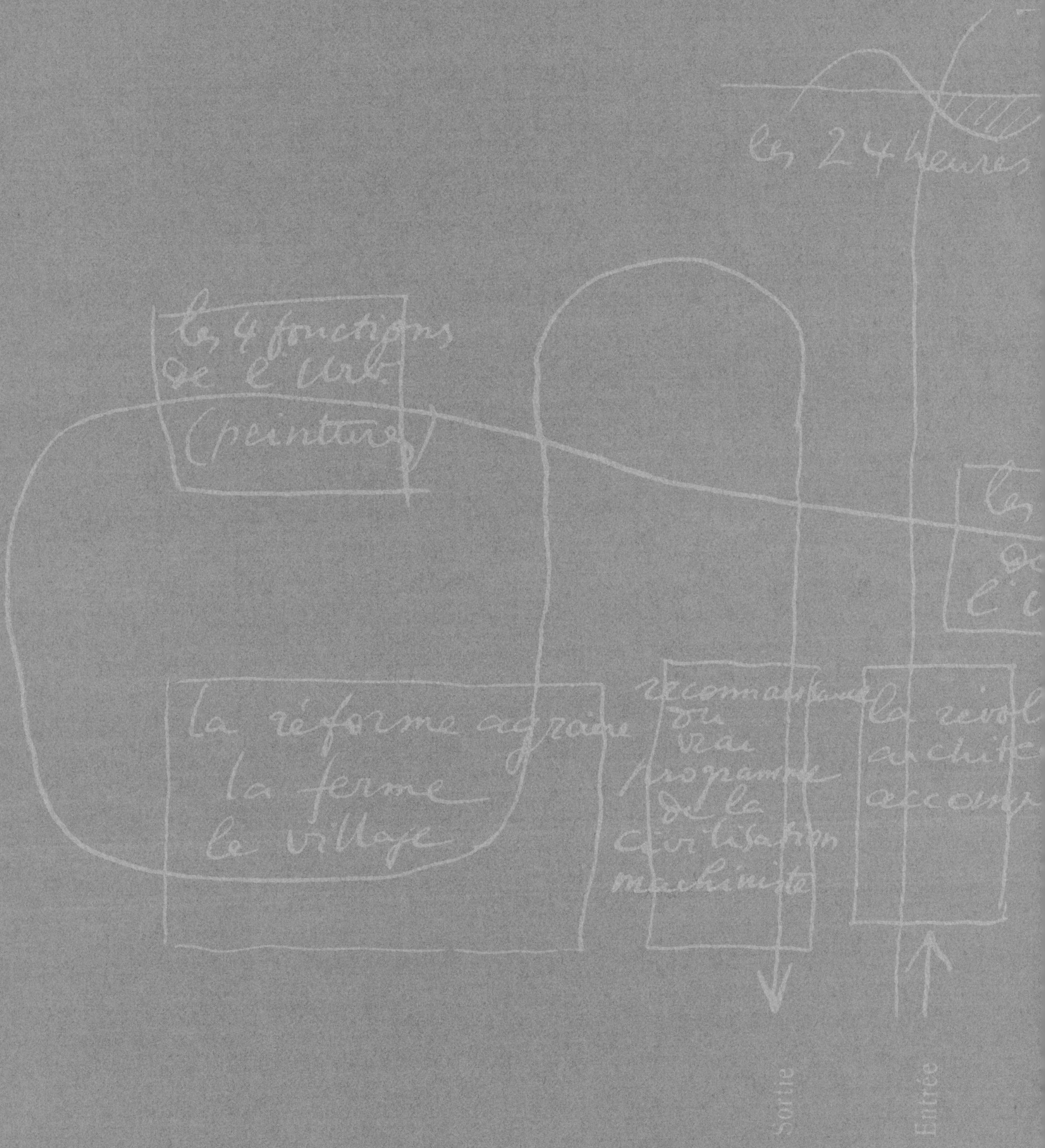

les 24 heures

les 4 fonctions
de l'Urb.

(peinture)

la réforme agraire
la ferme
le village

reconnaissance
du
vrai
programme
de la
civilisation
machiniste

les
de
l'u

la révol
architec
accom

Sortie

Entrée

Part 1 – Initiation

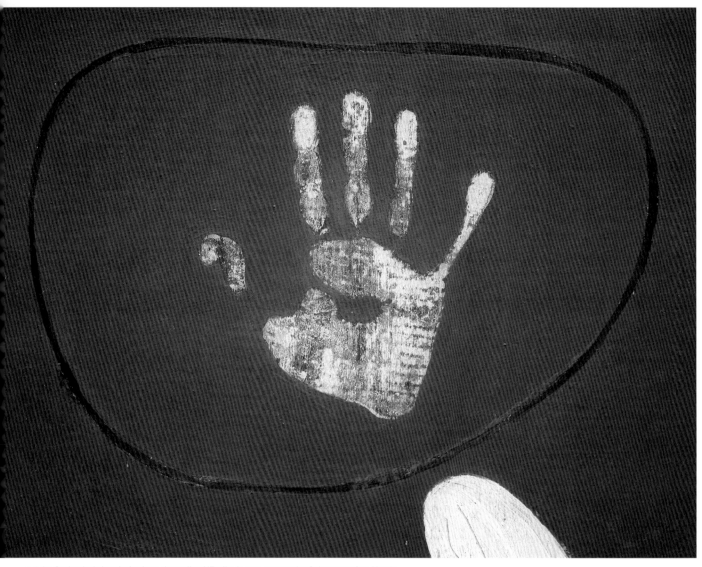

1.1 **Le Corbusier's handprint from the wall at L'Etoile de mer, next to the Cabanon at Cap Martin.**

1. Synchronisation of the Senses

Architecture is a series of successive events… events that the spirit tries to transmute by the creation of relations so precise and so over-whelming that deep physiological sensations result from them, that a real spiritual delectation is felt at reading the solution, that a perception of harmony comes to us from the clear-cut mathematical quality uniting each element of the work.[1]

The body of course plays a central role in all this. It would act as the vital intermediary in any transaction of knowledge between building and brain that would take place on the promenade. "I have a body like every-one else, and what I'm interested in is contact with my body, with my eyes, my mind."[2] Building on the ideas of Plato,[3] Le Corbusier believed that the primary means to influence thought was by influencing the body at a subconscious level,[4] the "joys of the body" being "interdependent to intellectual sensations."[5] In this way the "emotion leading to action" could then be felt in "our inner depths, before even the formulation of a theory".[6] Nowhere in architecture is the potential of bodily contact felt more readily than in the realm of detail, de-signed specifically to be touched or seen at close quarters – here "the architectural work enters the plane of sensitivity" and "We are moved".[7]

For Le Corbusier each person contained "a sounding board", a measure of harmony shared with "all phe-nomena and all objects of nature" leading us "to assume a unity of conduct within the universe".[8] The task of architecture was to respond to that inner sounding board and advance the cause of this "primal will" by eliciting a response from the body. This chapter therefore focuses upon the ways in which architecture could facilitate this process.

Rhythms of the Body

Central to the development of Le Corbusier's ideas on the relationship between the body and rhythm is the work of the unorthodox French art historian Elie Faure (1873–1937). In 1955 when compiling a list of his favourite books for reading on an aeroplane (including as usual Cervantes and Rabelais) Le Corbusier

---

1 Le Corbusier, *Precisions on the Present State of Architecture and City Planning* (Cambridge MA: MIT, 1991), p.160. Originally published as *Précisions sur un état présent de l'architecture et de l'urbanisme* (Paris: Crès, 1930).

2 Le Corbusier, *The Final Testament of Père Corbu* (New Haven: Yale University Press, 1997), p.120. Originally published as *Mise au Point* (Paris: Editions Forces-Vives).

3 As Plato observed "rhythm and harmony find their way into the inward places of the soul" resulting in a "true education of the inner being". Plato, *The Republic III*, in Scott Buchanan (ed.), *The Portable Plato* (Harmondsworth: Penguin, 1997), p.389.

4 Le Corbusier, *The Decorative Art of Today* (London: Architectural Press, 1987), p.167. Originally published as *L'Art décoratif d'aujourd'hui* (Paris: Editions Crès, 1925).

5 Arthur Rüegg (ed.), *Polychromie Architecturale: Le Corbusier's Colour Keyboards from 1931 to 1959* (Basel, Boston, Berlin: Birkhäuser, 1997), p.101.

6 Le Corbusier, *The Decorative Art of Today*, p.169.

7 Le Corbusier, *Precisions*, p.82.

8 Le Corbusier, *Towards a New Architecture* (London: Architectural Press, 1982), pp.192–193. Originally published as *Vers une Architecture* (Paris: Crès, 1923).

1.2 **Philips Pavilion exterior, Brussels International Exhibition (1958).**

thought of Faure. "I like Elie Faure, he anticipates, he appreciates, he understands."[9] Originally a friend of Amedée Ozenfant,[10] Faure was one of the original members of CIAM, the *Congrès Internationaux d'Architecture Moderne*. Le Corbusier owned a number of his books, some signed by the author himself.[11] Indeed Faure's student son worked with Pierre Jeanneret as part of his training.[12]

For Faure number, in the form of rhythm, had an important role in controlling human excesses and making a connection with "something which is perhaps God, but is in any case the gravitation of the skies".[13]

I shall not explain why mathematical and musical harmonies whose language is absolutely rigorous, act above all on the unconscious. Everyone knows the irresistible effect of music on the senses and the instantaneous setting off of spiritual rapture which is given to certain minds by the succession – automatic for them – of geometrical propositions and algebraic equations. Nor why artistic and biological harmonies, despite their vague language, act upon the conscious mind... here to mark the passage from the individual, overburdened with consciousness to the crowd's unconsciousness, ready to adopt unanimous new rhythms, a constant sensual rapture in mathematical settings impossible to grasp, although strictly rigorous... I would like for dance and above all cinema, to harmonise in the evolving unity of all these paradoxical relationships.[14]

9   Le Corbusier, *Sketchbooks Volume 3 1954–1957* (Cambridge MA: MIT, 1982), sketch 645.
10   J. Lowman, "Le Corbusier 1900–1925: The Years of Transition." Unpublished Doctoral Dissertation, University of London (1979), p.237.
11   Elie Faure, *Equivalences* (Paris: Robert Marin, 1951). Elie Faure, *Histoire de l'art. L'esprit des formes* (Paris: Germain Crès, 1927) with a dedication from the author to Jeanneret. Elie Faure, *Histoire de l'art*, vols. I, II, III, IV (Paris: Germain Crès, 1924) all in the Fondation Le Corbusier (hereafter referred to as FLC). Le Corbusier read *Equivalences* in March 1951. Le Corbusier, *Sketchbooks 2* (London: Thames and Hudson, 1981), sketch 372.
12   Lowman, "Le Corbusier 1900–1925", p.241.
13   Translated from Elie Faure, *Fonction du Cinéma: de la cinéplastique à son destin social* (Paris: Editions Gonthier, 1995), p.12. Originally published in 1953.
14   Ibid., pp.14–15.

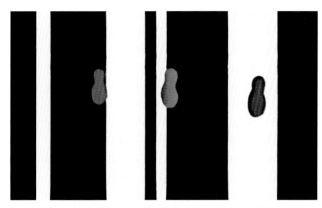

1.3 **A still from the film *Le Poème Electronique* by Le Corbusier (1958).**

Fascinated by the ways in which number could be used to make an impression upon the feelings, he believed that "architecture marks the passage of geometry from the architectural plane to that of the senses".[15] It is easy to see why Le Corbusier – who struggled with articulating the connection between the rhythms of architecture and those of the body – found Faure's ideas so affirmatory.

Scale

"The hours pass, the days pass, life passes. Events are all around us, we do not enter into them."[16] Le Corbusier meditated upon the cycles of nature – breath, the moon, the seasons, even menstruation, all of which provided evidence of the way in which human bodies are anchored to the world, giving scale to our endeavours. But then "everything was called in question. The limits of control were torn away… but the sun, imperturbable in its course, continued to mark the rhythm of our work."[17] It was the role of the architect to draw the reader's attention back to its fundamental course.

"Comprehensible in proportion to the steps which place us here, then take us there"[18] architecture should be "appreciated while on the move, with one's feet".[19] In Le Corbusier's opinion a central problem of the modern age was that it had tangled with human perception of space and time. "One day (a hundred years ago), man went from the immemorial speed of walking to the unlimited speed of machines."[20] The pace of the footprint is a key measure of space for Le Corbusier, its rhythm working in counterpoint against architecture. Nowhere is this seen more clearly than in the film of *Le Poème Electronique* capturing the performance of that same name that took place in the Philips Pavilion (Fig. 1.2) in Brussels as a collaboration between Le Corbusier, Edgar Varèse and Iannis Xenakis (1958). Although the actual performance, in which visitors to the exhibition moved through the uterine space of the pavilion itself – an initiation into space, music, colour and image – has never been repeated, it is possible to get some sense of the performance from the film and the book of that same name. The story of *Le Poème Electronique* is a dark one of civilisation, progress and its human cost. It begins with the tolling of a bell, a repeating refrain that gives a heartbeat to the piece. This rhythm is taken up by a pattern of footprints that repeats at intervals, those of a man, running in a direction counter to that of the film (Fig. 1.3). Other images appear at irregular intervals. Patterns proliferate, reinforced

15   From the preface written in 1935 by Faure for "Antonin Raymond, His work in Japan, 1920–35." Antonin Raymond, *An Autobiography* (Vermont: Charles E. Tuttle Company, 1973), p.150.

16   Le Corbusier, *When the Cathedrals were White* (New York: Reynal and Hitchcock, 1947), p.11. Originally published as *Quand les cathédrales étaient blanches* (Paris: Plon, 1937).

17   Ibid., p.xxii.

18   Le Corbusier, *Talks with Students* (New York, Princeton: 2003), p.46. Originally published as *Entretien avec les étudiants des écoles d'architecture* (Paris: Denoel, 1943).

19   Le Corbusier and Pierre Jeanneret, *Œuvre Complète Volume 2, 1929–34* (Zurich: Les Editions d'Architecture, 1995), p.24. Originally published in 1935.

20   Le Corbusier, *When the Cathedrals were White*, p.xxii.

by colour and echoed by repetitions in the music, climaxing with a series of piercing noises and an expelling whoosh.[21] Here Le Corbusier attempted to create a journey of sound, colour and light within the mathematical confines of the pavilion itself, playing in counterpoint to the footsteps of the initiate, like a vast three-dimensional orchestral score.

Music

A consciousness of the power of music permeates Le Corbusier's thinking on the promenade where "Proportions provoke sensations; a series of sensations like the melody in music".[22] Despite the fact that both his mother and brother were dedicated musicians, it was a young engineer and composer, Iannis Xenakis, working in Le Corbusier's atelier in the mid 1950s who did the most to translate Le Corbusier's theories into architecture.[23]

Le Corbusier asked Xenakis to apply the Modulor proportional system to the vertical struts of a glazing system in 1956, the result being the ondulatoire, or undulatory glass surface which first made its appearance at La Tourette.[24] It was repeated in a variety of late buildings, for example the Maison des Jeunes at Firminy (Fig. 1.4) and the Carpenter Centre where, as William Curtis observes, "especially on a curved plane, the ondulatoires allow a direct experience of their rhythm even to the static observer."[25]

Xenakis describes the development of the ondulatoire in lengthy musicological detail in an essay on the monastery in Volume 28 of the *Le Corbusier Archive*. "I found out the vertigo of combinatorics in architectural elements, after having experimented with them in music…"[26] A brief digression into Xenakis' music, particularly *Metastasis (spectral view, 1954)* with its accompanying film is worthwhile as it reveals much of relevance to this discussion. Metastasis is a medical term referring to the transfer of disease from one organ or part of the body to another. This, his first stochastic composition, was defined by Xenakis as a cure for what he felt to be the incoherence of serial music.

The film begins with what looks like heart blips on a monitor. Violins with occasional percussion enter in irregular rhythms. The screen fades into vertical striations. The blips start to widen accompanied by trumpets and then quieten again. The striations become horizontal, they emerge and fade in a heartbeat rhythm. Then little blips appear (flutes) that weave through the existing weft of sound. Although I have no qualifications to make any commentary on musical theory – the relationship between jazz, stochastic music and the work of Le Corbusier badly needs proper exploration – there is an important theme at work here that, I will argue, can be seen in Le Corbusier's promenades.[27] This is the conscious play of surprise, colour and tone against

21   A popular theme in artistic circles in the 1940s from Hollywood to Paris, writes Eisenstein, was the relationship between colour and music. Sergei Eisenstein, *The Film Sense* (London: Faber and Faber, 1977), pp.90–91. First published in 1943.
22   Le Corbusier, *Precisions,* p.133.
23   Le Corbusier, *Modulor 2* (London: Faber, 1955), p.321. Originally published as *Le Modulor II* (Paris: Editions d'Architecture d'Aujourd'hui, 1955).
24   Ibid., p.32.
25   Le Corbusier, *Œuvre Complète Volume 7, 1957–1965* (Zurich: Les Editions d'Architecture, 1995), p.100. Originally published in 1965.
26   Iannis Xenakis, "The Monastery of La Tourette" in H. Allen Brookes (ed.), *The Le Corbusier Archive, Volume XXVIII* (New York: Garland, 1983), pp.xi–xii. Hereafter referred to as Allen Brookes, *Archive XXVIII.*
27   F.P. Miller, A. F. Vendome, J. McBrewster, *Iannis Xenakis* (Mauritius: Alphascript, 2009).

1.4 **Ondulatoire glazing, Maison des Jeunes, Firminy (1965).**

the backdrop of the heartbeat, a play similar to that within *Le Poème Electronique*, pointing to a possible consistency of approach. Xenakis himself stated in his book *Formalised Music* that his was a compositional method that imitates natural phenomena "by finding a balance between order and chaos".[28] I would argue that this has much in common with Le Corbusier's architecture and that the unfolding experience of the promenade can be understood as a series of events and rhythms like those in a musical score.

The workings of the inner ear, this liquid source of balance, this vibrating receptacle of sound, were a source of considerable symbolic significance for Le Corbusier and provided inspiration for a series of studies known as the "acoustic" forms. Le Corbusier considered himself to be rather good at the manipulation of sound, though this is an aspect of his work that has received little considered attention. Certainly the dramatically long reverberation time experienced at La Tourette and the extraordinary silence of the Unité apartment are testament to his skill in this area. Clearly, given Le Corbusier's preoccupation with sound, and the important role sound plays in introducing spaces that cannot be seen, it should have played a significant role in his conception of the promenade, although there is no concrete evidence, beyond the buildings themselves, that this was the case.

Light

For Le Corbusier light served a number of important practical, sensorial and symbolic purposes, its choreography subject to endless refinement. "The key is light and light illuminates the shapes and shapes have an emotional power."[29] During the experience of the promenade the reader experiences highly sculpted sequences of light and dark.

Observe the play of shadows, learn the game... Precise shadows, clear cut or dissolving. Projected shadows, sharp. Projected shadows, precisely delineated, but what enchanting arabesques and frets. Counterpoint and fugue. Great music.[30]

His buildings need strong directional light to create shadow and to give necessary emphasis to the rhythm of the structure. He revelled in the drama of chiaroscuro, hence his enthusiasm for the photography of Lucien Hervé.

Le Corbusier knew full well how light could radically change the mood of a place. Indeed he wrote feelingly about the "calm of a well-lit bedroom or the anguish of a roomful of dark corners, enthusiasm or depression".[31]

When you are surrounded with shadows and dark corners you are at home only as far as the hazy edges of the darkness your eye cannot penetrate. You are not master in your own house. Once you have put ripolin on your walls you will be master of yourself. And you will want to be precise, to be accurate, to think clearly.[32]

To paint the walls white was to herald a new ascetic existence, one which would help the reader to concentrate on that which was really important in life.

As a young man Le Corbusier had eulogised about the Sanctuary of the "Mother of God" at Mount Athos and its "mysterious relationships of form and colour... *in the rhythm of the controlled light*" describing this as "a divine calling for the ancient builders!"[33] Gnostic faiths such as Manichaeanism (including Catharism with which Le Corbusier felt a particular affinity) focussed upon the relationship between the body and the soul and described the cosmos in terms of the relationship between night and day. According to Hans Jonas the symbolism of light and darkness is "everywhere in Gnostic literature".[34] Most usually associated with life and death, it could also symbolise good and evil and, indeed, the "other world" in relation to "this world" which was perceived to be dark and imperfect.[35] Such themes are at the core of Le Corbusier's dualistic thinking on the relationship between light and dark.

Games of illumination play a significant role in the writings of a number of writers much admired by Le Corbusier, most notably André Gide, Edouard Schuré and Guillaume Apollinaire, the last of whom – in the words of Virginia Spate – used ancient metaphors of light "revived by nineteenth-century poets to express the

29   Le Corbusier, *The Chapel at Ronchamp* (London: Architectural Press, 1957), p.27.
30   Ibid., p.47.
31   Ibid., p.75.
32   Le Corbusier, *The Decorative Art of Today*, p.188.
33   Le Corbusier, *Journey to the East* (Cambridge MA: MIT, 1987), p.183. Originally published as *Le Voyage d'Orient* (Paris: Parenthèses, 1887).
34   H. Jonas, *The Gnostic Religion* (Boston: Beacon Press, 1963), p.xvi. Originally published in 1958.

35   Ibid.

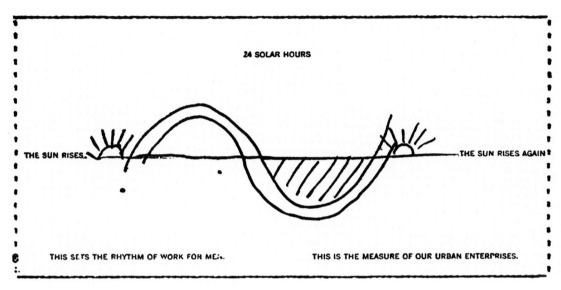

24 SOLAR HOURS

THE SUN RISES.

THE SUN RISES AGAIN

THIS SETS THE RHYTHM OF WORK FOR MEN.

THIS IS THE MEASURE OF OUR URBAN ENTERPRISES.

1.5 **Sign of the 24-hour day from Le Corbusier, *Quand les cathédrales étaient blanches* (1937).**

primordial unity of all matter and the aspiration of the soul to be reunited with light, the divine source of all being".[36] The initiatory journey, in this case based on Orpheus' journey into the darkness of the Underworld became, for Apollinaire, a metaphor for the poet's own quest for inner wholeness, an idea that Le Corbusier seems to have subscribed to fully.

The opposition of light and dark was of profound importance to Le Corbusier's life and work. It provides the focus of his sign for the 24-hour day (Fig. 1.5) which tracks the movements of the sun above and below the horizon – used for example, on the entrance stone of the Unité apartment block at Marseilles. "If, in the course of the mutation of the machine civilisation, I have been able to contribute something, as a person with some rationality and intelligence, as technician, as a thoughtful man, it will be this sign."[37] For Le Corbusier it was to be an object of meditation for those "whose mission it is to see clearly and to lead" and held within it the key to "habitation... knowing how to live! How to use the blessings of God; the sun and the spirit that He has given to men to enable them to achieve the joy of living on earth and to find again the Lost Paradise".[38] Slippages between the word light and the word knowledge are absolutely prevalent, light having a paramount role in the art of *savoir habiter*.[39] Seeing clearly is a recurrent theme in Le Corbusier's work. The lighting for the Assembly at Chandigarh would, for example allow the members "*to see clearly*, to decide world affairs and to take advantage of the optimism of the sun's rays".[40] It is only fitting therefore that the denouement of the promenade so frequently took the form of a dazzling fanfare of light.

---

36   V. Spate, *Orphism: the Evolution of Non-figurative Painting in Paris in 1910–14* (Oxford: Clarendon, 1979), p.63.
37   From introduction to Le Corbusier, *When the Cathedrals were White*, p.xvii.
38   Ibid.
39   See Todd Wilmert, "The ancient fire the hearth of tradition: Creation and Combustion in Le Corbusier's studio residences", *arq*, 10, 1 (2006), pp.57–78.
40   Le Corbusier, *Precisions*, p.161.

1.6 **Charles Edouard Jeanneret (Le Corbusier),** *Nature morte à la lanterne* (1922).

Colour

Elie Faure wrote in *Equivalences* of "mysterious accord between sensuality, sensibility and intelligence" which could be influenced through the orchestration of colour. Le Corbusier underlined these words in his copy of Faure's work.[41] In its initial stages his architecture would share the muted Mediterranean palate and uniform smoothness of his early Purist paintings (Fig. 1.6). Here, as at the housing scheme for Pessac, colour was used to give emphasis to some walls and to dilute the power of others. Colour would be used with equal care in Le Corbusier's later work, where light would be used to bring it into his buildings, either reflected off brightly painted surfaces – as at Ronchamp where light bounces of the red interior of the tower to create an intense rosy glow – or by means of coloured glass (Fig.1.7).

Colour was used symbolically on the promenade to influence mood and to assert or diminish the presence of particular architectural elements.[42] For example Le Corbusier recognised fully "the psychological importance of colour on the spirits of the patients" in the Venice Hospital scheme. In 1932 he developed a colour keyboard for the firm Salubra. This was "a system which makes it possible to establish a strictly architectural polychromy in the modern dwelling, one in accordance with nature and with the deep needs of each person".[43] "Colour… Mister Psychiatrist, is it not an important tool in diagnosis?" he wrote.[44]

Sensory Stimulation

Both form and texture were manipulated by Le Corbusier with the specific intention of moving and arousing the body. Given that his paintings were, for Le Corbusier, a source of architectural form, it follows that his buildings too would retain echoes of the body from which they were conceived. "I have a body like everyone else," wrote Le Corbusier, "and what I'm interested in is contact with my body, with my eyes, my mind."[45]

In 1928 he "threw open a window on the human figure"[46] in his painted work, expressing an uneasiness with abstraction because of a need "to keep contact with living beings".[47] Christopher Pearson makes the point that within Le Corbusier's domestic architecture a work of art was intended, amongst other things, to act as a "carefully sited anthropomorphic presence within the building, which could dramatise… the visitor's relationship to and participation in the architectural space by the creation of a sympathetic bond between visitor and sculpture" (Fig 1.8).[48] Similarly Le Corbusier would adopt anthropomorphic forms into his architecture in order to maximise its psychological impact on the visitor.

41   Elie Faure, *Equivalences*, p.18 in FLC. Similar sentiments were expressed by another of his favourite authors Henri Provensal, *L'Art de Demain* (Paris: Perrin, 1904), p.54 in FLC.

42   L.M. Colli, "La couleur qui cache, la couleur qui signale: l'ordonnance et la crainte dans la poétique corbuséenne des couleurs" in *Le Corbusier et la couleur* (Paris: Fondation Le Corbusier, 1992), pp.21–34.

43   Le Corbusier, "Claviers de couleurs" from the trade literature for Salubra reprinted in L.M. Colli, "Le Corbusier e il colore; I Claviers Salubra", *Storia dell'arte*, 43 (1981), p.283.

44   Ibid., p.107.

45   Le Corbusier, *The Final Testament of Père Corbu*, p.120. Originally published as *Mise au Point* (Paris: Editions Forces-Vives).

46   Le Corbusier, *A New World of Space* (New York: Reynal Hitchcock, 1948), p.16.

47   Ibid., p.21. See D. Neagele, "The Image of the body in the Œuvre of Le Corbusier" in *Architecture Landscape and Urbanism 9, Le Corbusier and the Architecture of Reinvention* (London: AA Publications, 2003), pp.16–39.

48   C.E.M. Pearson, "Integrations of Art and Architecture in the Work of Le Corbusier. Theory and Practice from Ornamentalism to the 'Synthesis of the Major Arts'". PhD thesis, Stanford University (1995), p.140.

1.7 **Window in the South wall of Notre-Dame du Haut, Ronchamp (1955).**

1.8 **A sculpture by Laurens giving human presence within the Villa Stein de Monzie,
Garches from the *Œuvre Complète*.**

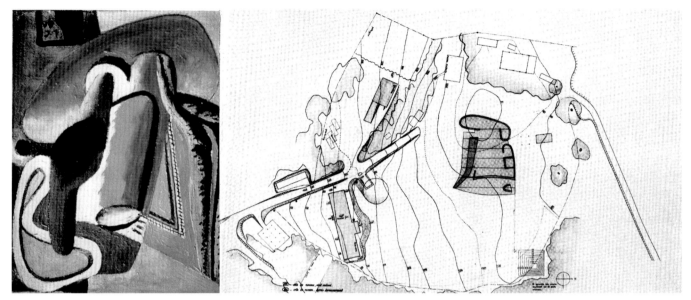

1.9 **Similarities between the plan of Notre-Dame du Haut, Ronchamp (1955), from Le Corbusier, *Œuvre Complète* and Le Corbusier, *Forme acoustique*, pastel on paper, New York (1946).**

"I believe in the skin of things, as in that of women," wrote Le Corbusier in *When the Cathedrals were White*[49] – a quotation that his friend Lucien Hervé reused in his own book on the architect, juxtaposed with an image of the gunite curves of the Chapel of Notre Dame du Haut Ronchamp, looking remarkably like skin seen at very close quarters.[50] Ronchamp is the most anthropomorphic of Le Corbusier's buildings, its plan (Fig. 1.9) based on Le Corbusier's acoustic form paintings which are themselves based on studies of women (Fig 1.10). Its curved, highly bodily forms were designed to awaken the senses, to remind us of the pleasures of touch and being touched.[51]

The human hand attains the status of fetish in the work of Le Corbusier – his handprint is a mark of emphatic presence and knowledge, a knowledge gained through touch, enabling the mind to learn how to feel through the eyes. Willing himself into a state of synaesthesia, Le Corbusier wrote that it was possible to "hear" the "music of visual proportion" of a building,[52] "taste" a column with his "eyes" and so on. His eyes awaken sensations in his mouth. His hands awaken his eyes as he wrote in *Le Poème de l'angle droit*:

Life is tasted through
the kneading of the hands
eyesight resides in
palpation[53]

Indeed he believed that "touch is a second kind of sight. Sculpture or architecture, when their forms are inherently successful, can be caressed; in fact, our hands are impelled towards them."[54] Not only are hands in contact with the fabric of a building – so are feet. A tacit hierarchy can be read, and indeed felt, through the finishes on the floor, intrinsic to the experience of the architectural promenade.

49 Le Corbusier, *When the Cathedrals were White*, p.14.
50 Lucien Hervé, *Le Corbusier The Artist/Writer* (Neuchâtel: Editions du Grifon, 1970), p.28.
51 J. Coll, "Structure and Play in Le Corbusier's Art Works", *AA Files* 31 (1996), pp.3–15.
52 Le Corbusier, *Modulor 2*, p.148.
53 Le Corbusier, *Le Poème de l'angle droit* (Paris: Editions Connivance, 1989). Section F3, Offering. Originally published in 1954.
54 Le Corbusier, p.59.

1.10 **Le Corbusier, *Icône 1* (1955).**

Conclusion

Believing that the body played a primary role in the assimilation of knowledge, Le Corbusier evolved a series of techniques to facilitate this process. Mixing from his palate of sensory experiences, rhythm, colour, light and touch, each subject to its own inner laws, he choreographed sequences of spaces that would elicit responses at the most visceral level. Eisenstein would refer to this process as the "Synchronisation of the Senses" with reference to the art of film.[55]

In Le Corbusier's early schemes regulating lines were used to send harmonious spatial messages to the senses.[56] In his later work the Modulor would assist in this task. Le Corbusier was always keen to stress the links between his system of proportion and that of the body, beauty "acting like sound waves on a resonator".[57] As a time keeping instrument the body had its own rhythm that would be enhanced and augmented by that of Le Corbusier's architecture. Light and dark would add a further beat to the choreography of the route whilst playing upon the reader psychologically through the power of symbols. This tympany of experiences would be backed up by sensory stimuli and, on some occasions, by the experience of fear, shocking the reader into focus. It would however be interspersed with periods of quietude for recovery and meditation when space takes centre stage.

---

55   See chapter entitled "Synchronisation of the Senses" in Eisenstein, *The Film Sense*, pp.60–91.
56   FLC 15589 shows the importance of regulating lines in the composition of the lower reaches of the Pavillon Suisse. FLC 15589 in Allen Brookes, *Archive*, *VIII*, p.289.
57   Le Corbusier, *Precisions*, p.156.

2.1 **Corridor in the nursery of the Unité, Firminy (1959).**

Time was always a serious pre-occupation for Le Corbusier – trained, as a young man like his father before him, in the art of enamelling watch cases (Fig 2.2). Indeed centre place was to be given to one of the first watches that he made in the "museum Corbu", in what was then the dilapidated remains of the Villa Savoye indicating its continued relevance to his work and thought.[1]

In the early decades of the twentieth century the very nature of time was being called into question not only in the arts – Marcel Duchamp's *Nude Descending a Staircase* (1912) being a very famous example – but in the sciences. It is no accident that Le Corbusier went out of his way to court the patronage of Albert Einstein. This chapter focuses on the framing of experiences in time and in space of what might be called – in movie terms – the cinematography and direction of the promenade.

Perspective

Despite the fact that the very idea of the promenade may have its origins in the Beaux Arts concept of "la marche"[2] Le Corbusier criticised the products of the Beaux Arts school for being built around perspectives that could only really be understood from one fixed viewing point. He wanted to create spaces that could be appreciated on the move – "it is while walking, moving from one place to another, that one sees how the arrangements of the architecture develop".[3] During his early career he became interested in the garden city movement, not just because it allowed people access to nature, but because of the varied and picturesque routes created across these spaces. At the same time he became an admirer of the work of the town planner Camillo Sitte, known for creating curved and oblique routes that would encourage exploration and surprise.[4]

First visited by Le Corbusier as a young man on his "journey to the east", the Acropolis revealed to him a multitude of lessons, on the power of geometry, on Platonic forms, on the possibilities of a Radiant architecture and, most significantly for this discussion, on the asymmetrical organisation of space.[5] He admired it for its subtle gradation of axes building up towards the experience of the Parthenon.[6]

1   J. Quetglas, *Le Corbusier, Pierre Jeanneret: Villa Savoye 'Les Heures Claires' 1928–1963* (Madrid: Rueda, 2004).
2   David Van Zanten, "Architectural Composition at the Ecole des Beaux-Arts from Charles Percier to Charles Garnier," in Arthur Drexler (ed.), *The Architecture of the Ecole des Beaux-Arts* (New York: Museum of Modern Art, 1977), p.163.
3   Le Corbusier and Pierre Jeanneret, *Œuvre Complète Volume 2, 1929–34* (Zurich: Les Editions d'Architecture, 1995), p.24. Originally published in 1935.
4   Camillo Sitte, *City Planning According to Artistic Principles* (London: Phaidon, 1965). Originally published in 1889. See Tim Benton "Urbanism" in *Le Corbusier: Architect of the Century* (London: Arts Council, 1987), p.201.
5   Significantly Sergei Eisenstein was himself an admirer of the Acropolis. Sergei Eisenstein, "Montage and Architecture" (c.1937), *Assemblage*, 10 (1989), p.117.
6   Le Corbusier makes reference to Choisy's *Histoire de l'architecture* in a note in the Carnet Paris Automne 1913, p.49 (Bibliothèque de la Ville de La Chaux-de-Fonds, 10-LC107 – 1038. Reprinted in J.K. Birksted, *Le Corbusier and the Occult* (Cambridge MA: MIT, 2009), p.26.

2.2 **Charles Edouard Jeanneret (Le Corbusier), watchcase (1906).**

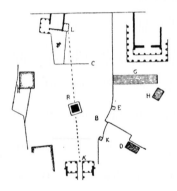

THREE REMINDERS TO ARCHITECTS

III

PLAN

THE ACROPOLIS

A view which shows the Parthenon, the Erechtheum, and the statue of Athena in front of the Propylea. It should not be forgotten that the site of the Acropolis is very up and down, with considerable variations in level which have been used to furnish imposing bases or plinths to the buildings The whole thing being out of square, provides richly varied vistas of a subtle kind ; the different masses of the buildings, being asymmetrically arranged, create an intense rhythm. The whole composition is massive, elastic, living, terribly sharp and keen and dominating.

2.3 **A plan and perspective view of the Acropolis, printed in *Towards a New Architecture* (1923) reprinted from the pages of Auguste Choisy's *Histoire de l'architecture* (1899).**

2.4 **"The Aquitania (Cunard Line)"** from *Towards a New Architecture* **(1923).**

It should not be forgotten that the site of the Acropolis is very up and down, with considerable variations in level which have been used to furnish imposing bases or plinths to the buildings. The whole thing, being out of square, provides richly varied vistas of a subtle kind; the different masses of the buildings, being asymmetrically arranged, create an intense rhythm. The whole composition is massive, elastic, living, terribly sharp and keen and dominating.[7]

A plan and perspective view of the Acropolis, taken from the pages of Auguste Choisy's *Histoire de l'architecture*[8] appear twice within the pages of *Towards a New Architecture*, once alongside the above words, thus reinforcing its importance in the development of the promenade (Fig. 2.3).[9]

Le Corbusier seems to have developed a repugnance for full frontal views of buildings. He admired the Acropolis because "you are able to get a three quarters view of" the Parthenon and the Erechtheum. It was his opinion that "architectural buildings should not all be placed upon axes, for this would be like so many people talking all at once".[10] It must be for this reason that all three-dimensional impressions of his early villas are on the oblique. Yet at the same time he retained a fondness for relentless space marching towards a central vanishing point. The image of "the Aquitania (Cunard Line)" in *Towards a New Architecture* provides a case in point (Fig. 2.4). "Architects note: the value of the long gallery or promenade – satisfying and interesting volume; unity in materials". The merit here is not from the surprise of unexpected events but from experience of walking through an extended cuboid of space with the sea on one side. A corridor, such as that of the Aquitania, can become a relentless trial to traverse yet it provides an important tool for the designer determined to wreak maximum drama from built space. For Eisenstein lengthy montage sequences expressing long distances from point to point were important in film making for making an impression of "solemnity".[11] Similarly the long gallery forms a spatial hiatus, a breathing place or clearing that allows for the better appreciation of complexity past and complexity to come.

7   Le Corbusier, *Towards a New Architecture* (London: Architectural Press, 1982), p.43. Originally published as *Vers une Architecture* (Paris: Crès, 1923).
8   Auguste Choisy, *Histoire de L'Architecture* (Paris: Édouard Rouveyre, 1899), pp.414–415. An illustration of the relevant pages appears in Birksted, *Le Corbusier and the Occult*, p.84.
9   Richard Etlin, "Le Corbusier, Choisy and French Hellenism: The Search for a New Architecture", *The Art Bulletin*, LXIX, 2, (1987), pp.264–278.
10   Le Corbusier, *Towards a New Architecture*, p.175.
11   Sergei Eisenstein, "Montage and Architecture", p.121.

2.5 **Drawing from *Towards a New Architecture* (1923).**

It is possible that Le Corbusier's drawings reflect what Vincent Scully has termed Le Corbusier's "monocular vision".[12] "I am a Cyclops in spite of myself, a nasty joke," wrote Le Corbusier referring to his lack of vision in one eye.[13] For Nicholas Fox Weber this is "why, in Le Corbusier's perspective drawings of the superhighway running through the new city, the vanishing point is much nearer than it would be in actuality, with the extreme foreshortening creating an artificial impression of energy and speed" (Fig. 2.5).[14] Whilst the inconsistencies in Le Corbusier's approach to perspective cannot all be put down to his physical limitations, his awareness of his own inability to judge distances must have given him an oddly heightened sensation of space.

There are undoubted tensions between Le Corbusier's desire to create varied and stimulating sequences of spaces and the gargantuan and relentless city plans that he posited during the 1920s. A series of examples in *Towards a New Architecture* show just how he would create spatial variation on a lengthy boulevard, but these tiny adjustments make little difference to the overall schema (Fig. 2.6). However in the *Plan Voisin* for Paris, several key monuments would be retained at ground level. Here we encounter the fourteenth century church of St Martin, next a "noble mansion", and beyond this "office buildings rising through the trees like many-facetted crystals".[15] The city is here experienced as a picturesque garden.

Axes are absolutely central to the Corbusian distribution of space, the cause of the axis allied to that of the "intention".

Arrangement is the grading of axes, and so it is the grading of aims, the classification of intentions. The architect therefore assigns destinations to his axes. These ends are the wall (the plenum, sensorial sensation) or light and space (again sensorial sensation).[16]

The axis did not have to exist in true space, games and illusion could be used to create false impressions, either to extend the axis in intriguing ways or to place emphasis on the main axis by suppressing the impact of less important things. Le Corbusier was very aware of what was possible in this regard. "By means of various fundamental elements which will be clearly shown in diagrams, I can demonstrate the illusion of plans, this illusion which kills architecture, ensnares the mind and creates architectural trickery…"[17] He wrote of the House of the Tragic Poet at Pompeii (Fig. 2.7):

Everything is on an axis, but it would be difficult to apply a true line anywhere. The axis is the intention, and the display afforded by the axis extends to the humbler things which it treats most skilfully (the corridors, the main passage, etc) by optical illusions.[18]

12   Interview Nicholas Fox Weber with Vincent Scully, 28 August 2002. N. F. Weber, *Le Corbusier: A Life* (New York: Knopf, 2008), p.186.
13   Letter to Ritter, Fondation Le Corbusier (hereafter referred to as FLC) R3-19-395 to 396, 21.6.22, Paris.
14   Weber, *Le Corbusier*, pp.186–187.
15   Le Corbusier and Pierre Jeanneret, *Œuvre Complète Volume 1, 1910–1929* (Zurich: Girsberger, 1943), p.119. Originally published in 1937.
16   Le Corbusier, *Towards a New Architecture*, p.173.
17   Ibid., p.167.
18   Ibid., p.175.

LE CORBUSIER, 1920. STREETS WITH SET-BACKS

Vast airy and sunlit spaces on which all windows would open. Gardens and playgrounds around the buildings. Simple façades with immense bays. The successive projections give play of light and shade, and a feeling of richness is achieved by the scale of the main lines of the design and by the vegetation seen against the geometrical background of the façades. Obviously we have here, as in the case of the City of Towers, a question of enterprise on a huge financial scale, capable of undertaking the construction of entire quarters. A street such as this would be designed by a single architect to obtain unity, grandeur, dignity and economy.

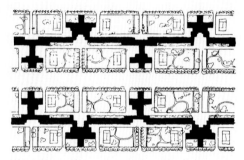

LE CORBUSIER, 1920. STREETS WITH SET-BACKS

2.6 **Drawing of the Ville Contemporaine (1922) from**
Towards a New Architecture (1923).

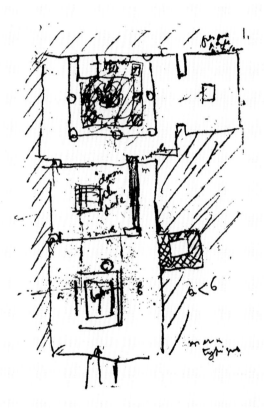

HOUSE OF THE TRAGIC POET, POMPEII

2.7 **Sketch of the House of the Tragic Poet, Pompeii from**
Towards a New Architecture (1923).

2.8 **Use of mirrors to create an illusion of space in the Villa Church (1929) from the *Œuvre Complète*.**

Hierarchy.
      1. The sign of the cross on the axis.
      2. The witness (the Tree).
      3. The presence of the Virgin Mary.
      Side by side happily in the scheme.
The protagonists are apparent,
clearly visible, they are not confused on an opposing axis.

2.9 **Le Corbusier's sketch of the altar at Notre-Dame du Haut, Ronchamp (1955) from
Le Corbusier, *The Chapel at Ronchamp*.**

2.10 **Kitchen, Villa Savoye (1929) from Le Corbusier's *Œuvre Complète*.**

Optical illusions are prevalent in Le Corbusier's work, for example in the Villa Church where mirrors are used to extend space beyond its boundaries (Fig. 2.8). Such highly Symbolist gestures invite questions, continually reminding the reader of the implications of space and its meaning.

Axial tension is a frequent occurrence in the work of Le Corbusier, the most notable example being that which occurs between the axis of the altar and the axis of the East door at Ronchamp, a composition that caused Le Corbusier a great deal of difficulty and "turmoil" (Fig. 2.9).[19] Commentary in the *Œuvre Complète* indicates that the climax of the church is at the point where the ceiling is at its highest, where there is most light. Normally this would occur above the altar, the absolute focus for any church, but in the case of Ronchamp the focus is above the East door pointing to a rather different agenda to that of most Christian Churches.[20] Here there is a conflict between two different axes and two different readings.

Having, as a young man, spent much time analysing the structural lines beneath Renaissance paintings, Le Corbusier would have been aware of what Eisenstein calls Durer and Leonardo's "deliberate use of several different perspectives and several vanishing points when it suited their purpose". Eisenstein notes that three vanishing points were used in Jan Van Eyck's *Arnolfini Wedding* (1434), "what a wonderful intensity of depth this painting gains thereby!"[21] and points out that in Leonardo's *Last Supper* the objects on the table have a different vanishing point from those in the room. Le Corbusier would play a similar trick with his famous image of the objects on the counter/altar of the Villa Savoye (Fig. 2.10) which are arranged in a form that suggests a vanishing point at odds with that of the room itself, in this way calling many things into question.

Eisenstein makes links between perspective and music in his paper "Synchronisation of the Senses" in which he includes a lengthy quote by René Guilleré linking jazz composition closely with a "new esthetic" which, I would argue, has much in common with Le Corbusier's aspiration:

19   Le Corbusier, *The Chapel at Ronchamp* (London: Architectural Press, 1957), pp.131–133. See also Flora Samuel, "A Profane Annunciation. The Representation of Sexuality in the Architecture of Ronchamp", *Journal of Architectural Education*, 53, 2 (1999), pp.74–90.

20   Ibid., pp.74–90.

21   Sergei Eisenstein, *The Film Sense* (London: Faber and Faber, 1977), p.84. Originally published in 1943.

2.11 **Villa Stein de Monzie, Garches (1928) from Le Corbusier's Œuvre Complète.**

Jazz seeks volume of sound, volume of phrase. Classical music was based on planes (not on volumes) – planes arranged in layers, creating an architecture of truly noble proportions… in jazz all elements are brought into the foreground. This is an important law that can be found in painting, in stage design, in films, and in poetry of this period. Conventional perspective with its fixed focus and its gradual vanishing point has abdicated…
In other words, in our new perspective – there is no perspective.[22]

In the case of jazz "different intensities, varying colour saturations now create the volumes".[23] What is less clear is how volumes might be created in architecture.

Colin Rowe and Robert Slutsky's well-known essay "Transparency: Literal and Phenomenal" has obvious implications for the development of the promenade as it is the interpenetration of its different stages that gives it its particular impetus. Rowe and Slutsky make their well-known distinction between "literal" transparency, for example the ability of a window to allow people to see through it, and "phenomenal" transparency "found when a painter seeks the articulated presentation of frontally aligned objects in a shallow, abstracted space",[24] using examples of Cubist and Post-Cubist painting to illustrate their argument. The works of Fernand Léger and his friend Le Corbusier are compared even though phenomenal transparency is far more difficult to achieve and still more to discuss in architecture than in painting.[25] Despite this Rowe and Slutsky identify a series of vertical planes working across the depth of the façades of the Villa Stein de Monzie at Garches (Fig. 2.11), a stratification that is continued internally.[26]

22   René Guilleré quoted in "The Synchronisation of the Senses" in Sergei Eisenstein, *The Film Sense*, p.81.
23   Ibid., p.81.
24   Colin Rowe, *The Mathematics of the Ideal Villa* (Cambridge MA: MIT, 1976), p.166.
25   Ibid.
26   Ibid., p.169.

It is quite difficult to understand what Rowe and Slutsky mean here. What creates a layer of strata in this complex vision of space. For me a layer is created when enough events – the projection of a balcony, a protrusion of the façade, the overhang of an awning, the projection of the mat well – extend the same distance from the main body of the house to suggest the existence of an implied vertical plane in space, "like knives for apportionate slicing of space".[27] Another implied layer is created further in, perhaps by the projection of wall panels and shutters, a further plane created by mullions and door frame and so on throughout the house. As the reader moves around the building each of the layers "claim attention". Certain expectations are set up by the experience of these planes, expectations that Le Corbusier then begins to manipulate resulting in "continuous fluctuations of interpretation" and the occasional prioritising of diagonal points of view.[28]

Rowe and Slutsky write of Le Corbusier's architecture in terms of the interaction of vertical and horizontal planes, yet it could be argued that space is experienced as a series of volumes. The distinction between planes and volumes was not to be taken lightly in the 1940s, as is made clear by Rene Guilleré who spoke of jazz space as a series of "successive volumes, acting on our sensitive being, provoking physical, physiological sensations" in contrast to the planar space of classical music.[29] It is my suggestion that there is a greater consciousness of planes in Le Corbusier's early work than in the later work which reads more successfully as a series of overlapping volumes.

Framing

Rather than successive planes or volumes, it is perhaps more useful to think of the promenade in terms of frames – planes with depth. Le Corbusier thought continually in terms of frames, frames to house people, frames to house views, frames to house his special collections, frames to store utilitarian things, frames to extend out into the environment drawing the influence of nature within. These frames, often proportioned by the Modulor, might be solid, diaphanous or implied – "A thought which reveals itself without word or sound, but solely by means of shapes which stand in a certain relationship to one another."[30] For Le Corbusier the creation of frames provided an opportunity to accentuate and celebrate his very particular view of space. In the opinion of Rowe, "the ability to charge depth with surface, to condense spatial concavities into plane, to drag to its most eloquent pitch the dichotomy between the rotund and the flat, is the absolutely distinguishing mark of Le Corbusier's later style".[31]

Le Corbusier's frames could be heavily emphasised or minimally detailed. A heavy frame creates a full stop in space, an event or a ritual. A minimal frame creates spatial flow – a unity between the frame and that which is being framed. Chamfers, the internal flanges of the frame, can be used to create illusion. Further, and most significantly for this argument, holes and projections created what Le Corbusier called "a back and forth

---

27 Ibid., p.175.
28 Ibid., p.170.
29 René Guilleré quoted in "The Synchronisation of the Senses", p.75.
30 Le Corbusier, *Towards a New Architecture*, p.187.
31 Colin Rowe, *The Mathematics of the Ideal Villa*, p.196.

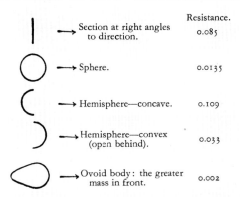

		Resistance.
Section at right angles to direction.		0.085
Sphere.		0.0135
Hemisphere—concave.		0.109
Hemisphere—convex (open behind).		0.033
Ovoid body : the greater mass in front.		0.002

The cone which gives the best penetration is the result of experiment and calculation, and this is confirmed by natural creations such as fishes, birds, etc. Experimental application : the dirigible, racing car.

2.12 **Diagram from *Towards a New Architecture* (1923) showing the air resistance of particular forms.**

movement",[32] the element of dynamism so central to the promenade. False right angles cause inflection and mystification.[33] This must have been why he took such care with the framing of his own paintings, and indeed the covers of his books.

Paintings, particularly murals, were in his later work used to dissolve walls, to bring about an alternative reality, a sudden and surprising pocket of space where before there was none. They represent alternative promenades into the world of the imagination, adding to the richness of the one perceived in real space. As well as providing a focus for meditation the blank panel, the negation of the frame, offers a static counterpoint to the shifting spaces and games of meaning that are so characteristic of Le Corbusier's architecture. Jerzy Soltan wrote disdainfully of working in offices "'after Corbu' time" when "any void, any hole, began to be glorified as INEFFABLE SPACE"[34] with no real understanding of its meaning. From this statement it can be inferred that the framing of ineffable space must have been a subject of discussion between Le Corbusier and his assistants and that the frames and voids in his work were fraught with intention.

Resistance

In *Towards a New Architecture* Le Corbusier provides a diagram showing cross sections through a variety of shapes together with statistics about the amount of air resistance each one induces (Fig.2.12). This is accompanied by press cuttings on motor cars and is a meditation on aerodynamics, the creation of the best shapes to induce speed.[35] Although the science may be antiquated one thing that becomes clear from the diagram is that a concave surface causes the greatest air resistance, the greatest inertia, closely followed by the flat surface. The "cone which gives the best penetration" is the "ovoid body" with "the greater mass in front", a

32   Le Corbusier, *Precisions* (Cambridge MA: MIT, 1991). Originally published as *Précisions sur un état présent de l'architecture et de l'urbanisme* (Paris: Crès, 1930), p.73.

33   See for example Colin Rowe, "La Tourette" in *The Mathematics of the Ideal Villa*, p.192.

34   J. Soltan, "Working with Le Corbusier" in Allen Brookes, *Archive XVII*, pp. ix–xxiv (p.xiv).

35   For a discussion of the gendered nature of the appreciation of speed see Enda Duffy, *The Speed Handbook: Velocity, Pleasure, Modernism* (Duke University Press, 2009).

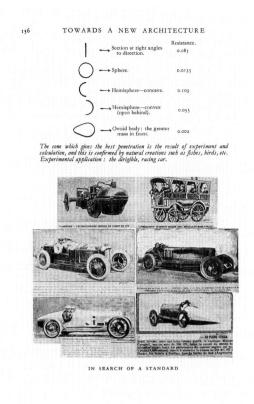

Resistance.

→ Section at right angles to direction.   0.085

→ Sphere.   0.0135

→ Hemisphere—concave.   0.109

→ Hemisphere—convex (open behind).   0.033

→ Ovoid body: the greater mass in front.   0.002

The cone which gives the best penetration is the result of experiment and calculation, and this is confirmed by natural creations such as fishes, birds, etc. Experimental application: the dirigible, racing car.

IN SEARCH OF A STANDARD

THE PARTHENON

Phidias in building the Parthenon did not work as a constructor, engineer or designer. All these elements already existed. What he did was to perfect the work and endue it with a noble spirituality.

2.13 **Air resistance diagram in context** *Towards a New Architecture* **(1923).**

discovery that is confirmed by "natural creations such as fishes, birds, etc".[36] This diagram appears across the page from a close-up detail along the porch of the Parthenon which makes the connection between cone and column in many ways explicit (Fig.2.13). My suggestion is that Le Corbusier knowingly used this information, which some might say is instinctual, to carve paths of least resistance through his buildings.

This has particular relevance to a discussion of pilotis or columns, a vital part of Le Corbusier's toolkit for the moulding of space. For Rowe the circular section "tended to push partitions away from the column" which meant that it did not aid the delineation of structural cells. It "offered a minimum of obstruction to the horizontal movement of space" and "tended to cause space to gyrate around it".[37] Other shapes of piloti were used to solicit or suppress a feeling of spatial flow.

Later on in the pages of *Towards a New Architecture* Le Corbusier acknowledged the importance of context in the "density" of forms – note here we are moving away from the scientific "resistance" to something far more subjective. A form may seem more dense if surrounded by nothingness. Both material and shape here come into play: "Then there is the sensation of density: a tree or a hill is less powerful and of a feebler density than a geometrical disposition of forms. Marble is denser both to the eye and to the mind, than is wood, and so forth. Always you have gradation."[38] There are echoes here of the kinds of concerns that Le Corbusier and Ozenfant expressed through their Purist paintings, where the subject matter was left simple to make

36   Le Corbusier, *Towards a New Architecture*, p.136.
37   Colin Rowe, *The Mathematics of the Ideal Villa*, p.145.
38   Le Corbusier, *Towards a New Architecture*, p.177.

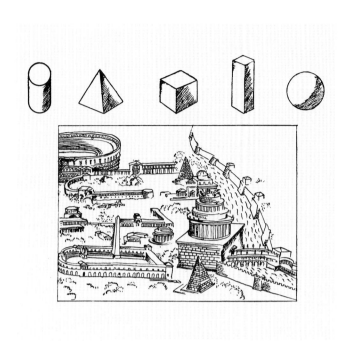

2.14 **"Simple masses" from *Towards a New Architecture*.**

2.15 **Compelling space. The ramp of the nursery in the Unité d'Habitation, Marseilles (1952), from *Les Maternelles*.**

the results of their forensic exploration of the potential of form more pronounced (Fig. 1.6). Colour would add to the effect: "The meeting of pale green or of white with brown provokes a suppression of volume (weight) and amplifies the deployment of surfaces (extension)." All of this would carry extreme "psychological power" and an "intense lyricism".[39] "Spaces, distances and forms, interior space and interior forms, interior route and exterior forms and exterior spaces – quantities, weights, distances, atmosphere, it is with these that we work".[40]

Within the overall dramatic structure, parts of the promenade are designed to make the reader stop and think. Usually these places take the form of a square which is sometimes expressed through a change of floor finish or an overhead network of beams. Le Corbusier recognised the archetypal attraction of certain forms (Fig. 2.14) and their ability to confer on a space a sense of the sacred.

The corollary of static space is compelling space – space which incites movement (Fig. 2.15). Often views, distant light and transparency assist in the task of driving the reader on. The direction of structural lines, for example of beams in the ceiling, force an onward view. Compelling space may not always be a pleasant place to be as its indeterminate nature, cold materials and absence of light encourage departure.

Le Corbusier favoured a limited family of structural types, each of which would have important ramifications for the unfolding of the promenade. "From the very start the plan implies the methods of construction to be used."[41] The system that was to have the greatest longevity was the domino frame, which first entered his

---

39   Le Corbusier and Pierre Jeanneret, *Œuvre Complète Volume 1*, p.85.
40   Le Corbusier, *Precisions*, p.71.
41   Le Corbusier, *Towards a New Architecture*, p.166.

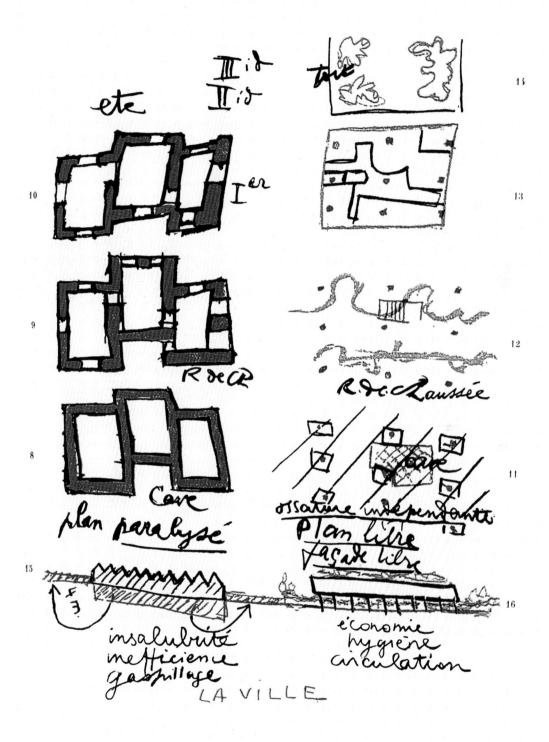

2.16 **Sketch from** *Precisions* **showing the benefits of the domino frame.**

work in 1914 (Fig. 2.16).[42] Here a floor slab, a first floor slab and a roof garden slab are linked by a simple dog leg stair and supported on slim columns. The façade and the walls have relinquished their former structural role giving them the freedom to be positioned at the will of the architect. Colin Rowe wrote of the Maison Domino and its offspring the Villa Savoye as being "symbols of emancipation" which carry implications of "social liberty".[43] Its development underpins Le Corbusier's advocacy of the "five points of a new architecture" – pilotis, horizontal windows, free façade, free plan and roof garden, the various aspects of which will be touched upon in the course of this argument.[44] The free plan was highly desirable for an architect who wanted maximum licence for the choreography of space. Such "holy Corbusierian principles" on the words of Jerzy Soltan "in turn expressed a variety of others…"[45]

Time and Progress

Time, that most resistant and unforgiving of entities, is of course implicated in all this.[46] The sign of the 24-hour day (Fig. 1.5) was designed as a "measuring instrument" mapping out the rhythms of nature, whilst at the same time delineating the scale of things in space. The sign is closely related to another of Le Corbusier's favourite laws, that of the meander which is very like the 24-hour day sign rotated by 90 degrees (Fig. 2.17). Charting the erosive journey of a river over the years, the loops become so extreme that the river cuts across them returning to a straight course. This sign in turn seems to have some relationship with the erratic path of donkeys (and women) identified with fondness by the young Le Corbusier on his "journey to the East". The message here is that there is underlying method in this rather instinctual method of perambulation.[47] In *The City of Tomorrow* he compares the straight path taken towards a fixed destination made by man "because he has a goal" with that of the donkey who zig-zags along, thinking a little, avoiding holes, negotiating with the slope, finding patches of shade (Fig. 2.18).[48] This is followed by a rumination on the right angle, which for Le Corbusier represented two different modes of being – the horizontal and the vertical. The idea that both forms of progress are necessary, the straight line of the man and the meander of the donkey, fits well into the genealogy of Le Corbusier's thinking on progress.[49]

One diagram in *Œuvre Complète Volume 3* set within a piece entitled "Meditations on Ford" is instructive as it represents Le Corbusier's view of evolution which he describes in the accompanying text. Here a sinuous line in blue crayon represents research and individual investigation. A similar line, this time in red, denotes "precedents, group activities, large and small; collaboration, co-operation, enthusiasm, sacred delirium…" (Fig. 2.19).[50] The process of discovery and progress is an undulating spiral working from individual to collective

---

42 For a discussion of the possible origins of the domino frame see William Curtis, *Le Corbusier: Ideas and Forms* (Oxford: Phaidon, 1986), p.42.

43 Colin Rowe, *The Architecture of Good Intentions* (London: Academy Editions, 1994), p.57. The same cannot be said of its usage in modern day office plans.

44 Le Corbusier and Pierre Jeanneret, *Œuvre Complète Volume 1*, pp.128–129.

45 Soltan, "Working with Le Corbusier", p.xvi.

46 For a discussion of the space time relationship see Juhani Pallasmaa, *Eyes of the Skin* (London: Wiley, 2005), p.21.

47 See Flora Samuel, *Le Corbusier Architect and Feminist* (London: Wiley/Academy, 2004) for an examination of his attitude to women.

48 For a discussion of the lineage of the zigzag path in Le Corbusier's work see Stanislaus von Moos, "Voyages en Zigzag" in Stanislaus von Moos and Arthur Rüegg (eds.), *Le Corbusier Before Le Corbusier* (Yale: New Haven, 2002), pp.23–53.

49 Le Corbusier *The City of Tomorrow* (London: Architectural Press, 1987), p.3 and p.13. Originally published as *Urbanisme* (Paris: Editions Arthaud, 1925).

50 Le Corbusier, "Méditation sur Ford" in Le Corbusier and Pierre Jeanneret, *Œuvre Complète Volume 3, 1934–38* (Zurich: Les Editions d'Architecture, 1995), p.16, p.24. Originally published in 1938.

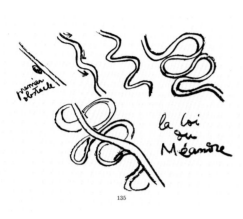

2.17 **The law of the meander from** *Precisions*.

2.18 **Sketch of donkeys from** *Poésie sur Alger* **(1950)**.

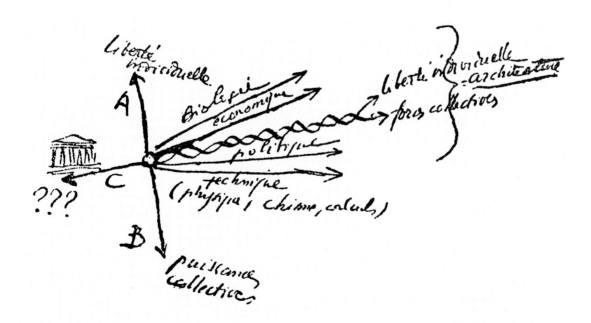

2.19 **Spiral of progress from** *Œuvre Complète.*

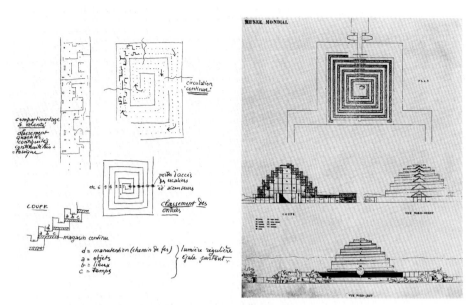

Le Musée Mondial: Le visiteur pénètre dans le musée par le haut. Trois nefs se déroulent parallèlement, côte à côte, sans cloison pour les séparer.
20) Entrée, 21) Centrum, 26) Ascenseurs, 27) Musée, 28) Rampe spirale, 30) Espace centrum, 43) Magasins, 44) Belvédère et entrée dans le musée.

2.20 **Le Musée Mondiale (1929) an early spiral museum project from the *Œuvre Complète*.**

and back again, like the swirling red spiral culminating in a pair of pleading hands that adorns the inner surface of the ceremonial door at Ronchamp. It also underpins the square spiral form of the Museum of Knowledge that appears repeatedly across Le Corbusier's career (Fig. 2.20).[51] Research and initiation would never be a straight path. Pitfalls and setbacks would always be necessary to proceed,[52] yet "men have always tried to lift themselves up, to climb as high as possible".[53]

In a domestic setting the promenade is of course something to be traversed again and again. Initiation, like the spiral view of evolution so fixed in Le Corbusier's mind, would be an iterative process. Each experience of the promenade – under different lighting conditions, at different times of year, in different frames of mind – would build upon the last, embedding its message of *savoir habiter* in the subconscious of its inhabitants.

The idea of life as a maze or a labyrinth here comes into play (Fig. 2.21). Le Corbusier was fascinated by the idea of Theseus' labyrinth built by Daedalus according to the numerical laws of the Egyptians.[54] He would have been fully aware of the ideas of the Mediaeval Compagnon builders who set labyrinths into the floors and walls of cathedrals as emblems of their geometric expertise.[55] His own buildings are in some ways a contemporary counterpart to this process. For Antoine Moles, a modern day Compagnon, "the alchemical labyrinth is the image of life with all its uncertainties and deceptions" – the labyrinth, like the endless museum, is a symbol of the way into knowledge.[56]

51   Le Corbusier and Pierre Jeanneret, *Œuvre Complète Volume 3*, p.46.
52   See Le Corbusier, *Nature morte geometric* (1930) for a significant use of the spiral in his painted work. See also Anthony Moulis, "Le Corbusier, the Museum Projects and the Spiral Figured Plan", *espace.library.uq.edu.au/eserv/.../Antony_Moulis_Le_Corbusier.pdf accessed 30 December 2009*.
53   Le Corbusier, *When the Cathedrals were White*, p.65.
54   André Gide, *Thésée* (Paris: Gallimard, 1946), p.62. In 1951 Le Corbusier read André Gide's *Thésée* with great interest. Le Corbusier, *Sketchbooks Volume 4*, sketch 62.
55   A. Moles, *Histoire des Charpentiers* (Paris: Librairie Gründ, 1949) in FLC.
56   "Le labyrinthe alchimiste est l'image de la vie avec ses incertitudes et ses déceptions". Moles, *Histoire des Charpentiers*, p.73, in FLC.

2.21 **"Labyrinth" from *Le Poème de l'angle droit*** (1955).

Rowe makes the astute observation of the Villa Stein de Monzie at Garches that "there are statements of a hierarchical ideal; there are counter statements of an egalitarian one".[57] At the same time, I would suggest, there is a conflict between the hierarchical *promenade architecturale* and the use of unhierarchical type detail. There is no crescendo in ingenuity, complexity or richness of materials as you move up through the building. In fact the opposite could be said to be the case, great care being taken on the design of the entrance and its associated spaces. The same tension is implicit in the iconostasis of the *Le Poème de l'angle droit* which is read from the top and finishes at the base, although its tree-like form suggests a reading which is diametrically opposite. Here is an example of the cyclical imperative that is so characteristic of his work (Fig. 2.22). The last square at the bottom of the iconstasis shows Le Corbusier's hand holding charcoal or carbon. It is for him "the answer and the guide",[58] simultaneously beginning and end, blackened yet humming with the potential of alchemical *nigredo*, a diamond in waiting. The cross drawn by the carbon, echoing the compass in the top square diametrically above it, extends in the vertical dimension towards the realm of the gods. There are two journeys here, cycling like the sign of the 24-hour day. Ignasi de Solà-Morales notes of

57   Colin Rowe, *The Mathematics of the Ideal Villa*, p.12.
58   Le Corbusier, *Le Poème de l'angle droit* (Paris: Editions Connivance, 1989), section G3, "Outil". Originally published in 1955.

the promenade that it is "time organised from the linear viewpoint".[59] This is certainly true, but is it a one-way route? Such paradoxes are integral to Le Corbusier's work and contribute to its potency.

Conclusion

The promenade acts as an allegory of life and its possibilities, encompassing Le Corbusier's view of evolution and progress, a constant incitement to live life to the full. He drew upon a range of techniques to highlight the experience of space and time in his work. These included perspective, axes, and frames as well as the use of particular forms that would create flow or cause resistance, altering the passage of movement along the way.

Josep Quetglas observes that "a continuous, linear form of time, like the time of calendars and narration, is incapable of recording the arrhythmic chain of events, the zigzagging, multidirectional turmoil, full of remorse and securities, the backward leaps and compelling prophecies" that happen in the course of any architectural project.[60] Yet Le Corbusier himself wrote very specifically about the choreography of the promenade, as though it was something with a particular chronology. There is constant chronological impetus in the work of Le Corbusier, but it is an impetus that he plays with and subverts at every possible opportunity.

59   Ignasi de Solà-Morales, *Differences: Topographies of Contemporary Architecture* (Cambridge MA: MIT, 1997), p.68. I am grateful to Jeremy Till for alerting me to this point.

60   Josep Quetglas, *Le Corbusier*, p.66

2.22 **Iconostasis of** *Le Poème de l'angle droit* **(1955).**

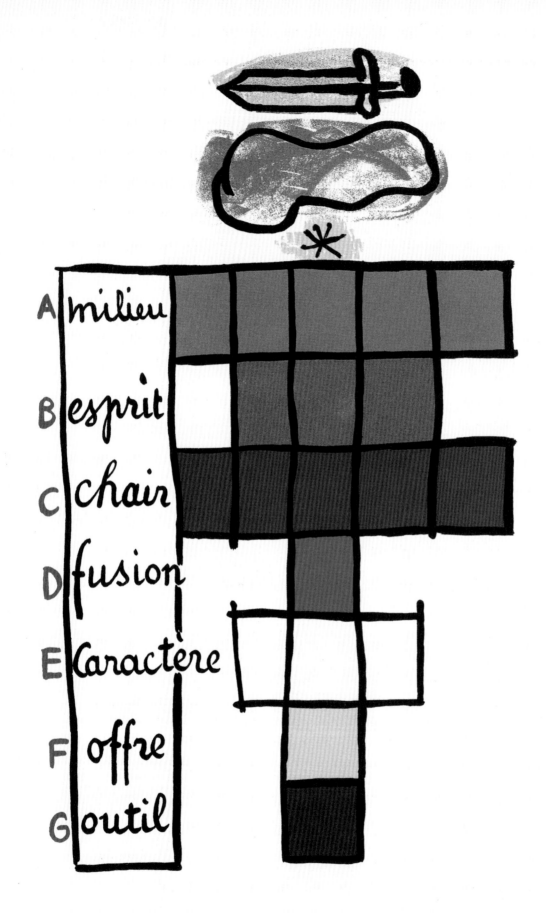

3.1 Iconostasis of *Le Poème de l'angle droit* (1955).

But I will only allow a poem made of "freestanding words". I want a poem made of solid words with defined meanings and a clear syntax.[1]

During his early career Le Corbusier developed a "passion" for analysing and organising into new groupings "objects that provoke a poetic reaction".[2] Often highly disparate in origin, these would be positioned strategically around the home evoking the household gods, the lares and penates of the villas in Pompeii that Le Corbusier visited as a young man.

The *technique of grouping* is in some ways a manifestation of the modern sensibility in the consideration of the past, of the exotic, or of the present. To recognise the "series", to create "unities" across time and space, to render thrilling the view of things where mankind has inscribed its presence.[3]

He here italicises the words "technique of grouping" emphasising its existence as a specific method which, I argue, has implications for the development of the promenade, itself a grouping of experiences[4] – "you classify and put events into hierarchies, you give them purposes".[5] The last chapter focussed on the framing of experiences in time and space, in filmic terms, the cinematography of the promenade. This chapter focuses on the narrative and the way that it is put together – the territory of the editor and the scriptwriter. It will describe the thinking behind of the initiatory route from dark to light that features so prominently in Le Corbusier's work. These range from the cold-blooded use of rhetorical tools of manipulation, through techniques of montage and Surrealism to more arcane versions of order such as that inscribed within the tenets of Orphism.

The task of a museum or gallery curator is to have a strong vision of the purpose of an exhibition.[6] Then, in order to make the vision happen, he or she needs to create a set of rules, or a methodology that will give order and boundaries to the collection to be displayed. "The museums are a recent creation and previously there were none. In their tendentious incoherence the museums provide no model; they can offer only the elements of judgments," wrote Le Corbusier.[7] To this end his friend Max Bill wrote in the *Œuvre Complète*

1   "Ou en est l'architecture?" in Le Corbusier et Pierre Jeanneret, I serie, *L'Architecture Vivante*, n.d., quoted in Tim Benton, *The Villas of Le Corbusier 1920–1930* (London: Yale, 1987), p.192.

2   Ibid., p.70.

3   Le Corbusier and Pierre Jeanneret, *Œuvre Complète Volume 3, 1934–38* (Zurich: Les Editions d'Architecture, 1995), p.157. Originally published in 1938.

4   Le Corbusier and Pierre Jeanneret, *Œuvre Complète Volume 1, 1910–1929* (Zurich: Girsberger, 1943), p.52. Originally published in 1937.

5   Interview by Le Corbusier with Robert Mallet, 1951 (extract from Entretiens. Le Corbusier, INA Archives, cassette, Editions Didaklée/INA, 1987) in Gilles Ragot and Mathilde Dion, *Le Corbusier en France: projets et réalisations* (Paris: Le Moniteur, 1997), p.175. Quoted in Caroline Maniaque, *Le Corbusier and the Maisons Jaoul* (New York: Princeton University Press, 2009), p.25.

6   For a discussion of the curation of architectural exhibitions see Jean-Louis Cohen, "Exhibitionist Revisionism: Exposing Architectural History", *The Journal of the Society of Architectural Historians* 58, no.3 (1999). Also Deyan Sudjic, Penny Sparke, Adrian Forty, Shumon Basar, Peter Cachola Schmal, Nick Barley, Jane Thomas, *Representing Architecture. New Discussions: Ideologies, Techniques, Curation* (London: Design Museum, 2008). p.41–74.

7   Le Corbusier, *The Decorative Art of Today* (London: Architectural Press, 1987), p.13. Originally published as *L'Art décoratif d'aujourd'hui* (Paris: Crès, 1925).

La porte d'entrée de 30 m² (plan en forme de lentille pivotant sur son axe médian)

La porte ouverte

3.2 **Entrance of the Pavillon des Temps Nouveaux, (1937) from the *Œuvre Complète*.**

that the Pavillon des Temps Nouveaux (1937) was designed to be polemical, "a challenging piece of cultural propaganda" with "no pretentions toward the monumental".[8] All Le Corbusier's other exhibitions err in a similar direction. If lacking in "unity" or a "great dominating idea" they would be of "no lasting value".[9] Important considerations in this scheme were the "management of a varied architectural promenade, the creation of contrasting volumes" and the "'widening of routes destined for the crowd… to give a succession

8   Le Corbusier and Pierre Jeanneret, *Œuvre Complète Volume 3*, p.12.
9   Ibid., p.11.

3.3 **Exit of the Pavillon des Temps Nouveaux, (1937) from the *Œuvre Complète*.**

of uninterrupted diverse views, intimate or monumental" (Fig. 3.2).[10] On exit via the main hall the visitor would be challenged by the following words: "this pavilion is dedicated to the people to understand, to judge and to claim back" (Fig. 3.3).[11]

For Le Corbusier "the true museum is one that contains everything, one able to give the whole picture of the past age". Only by containing everything could a museum "be truly dependable and honest... its value would lie in the choice that it offered, whether to accept or reject; it would allow one to understand the reasons why things were as they were, and would be a stimulant to improve on them. Such a museum does not yet exist."[12] Le Corbusier knew that by presenting a selected set of images or things he was creating an argument for a particular kind of existence. Further, given that one of his stated aims was to help people to understand, it follows that his collections the products of his curatorship must have been subject to clear guidelines and that events and artefacts experienced through the promenade were, wherever possible, purposefully arranged.

Rhetoric

Rhetoric was a further tool used by Le Corbusier to structure the arguments that he assembled in his lectures. It was used to persuade his audience to his way of thinking as Tim Benton has convincingly illustrated in *Le Corbusier and the Rhetoric of Modernism*.[13] Rhetoric follows a clear set of rules. According to Aristotle the philosopher searches for the truth which is founded on certain premises following the strict rules of logic, conforming approximately to the following stages.[14]

a.   Exordium – exposition
b.   Narratio – development
c.   Propositio – summation
d.   Argumentatio – argument
e.   Conclusio – conclusion[15]

---

10   Ibid., p.160.
11   Ibid., p.169.
12   Le Corbusier, *The Decorative Art of Today*, p.13.
13   Tim Benton, *Le Corbusier conférencier* (Paris: Editions le Moniteur, 2007), p.26. Published in English as *Le Corbusier and the Rhetoric of Modernism* (Basel, Boston, Berlin: Birkhäuser, 2009).
14   Aristotle, *Poetics* (c.4bc) translation by Malcolm Heath (London: Penguin, 1996).
15   J. H. Freese, *Aristotle, The Art of Rhetoric* (London: Loeb Classic Library, 1926).

3.4 **"The tribune and acoustic shell" at the Pavillon des Temps Nouveaux (1937) from the** *Œuvre Complète*.

Rhetoric could take different forms depending upon the orator's assessment of the audience's level of understanding.[16] A non-expert audience would be incapable of following the underpinning methodology of the argument – indeed there was absolutely no point in using arguments that the listener would not understand or fully appreciate. In such cases logic could be used to facilitate the art of persuasion.

Benton illustrates the subtle and "tendentious" game played by Le Corbusier to gain the sympathy of his audience.[17] Put simply his ploy was to flatter his listeners, to bring them on side (exordium), before making a no holds barred critique of their country, buildings or lifestyle (narratio) and before then suggesting a solution (proposition) using his own theories, giving concrete examples for things that might seem very abstract (demonstration), usually finishing with examples of his own work (conclusio).[18] Le Corbusier himself was fully aware of what he called "the breathtaking crossings of logic", almost as though he was aware of their intrinsic flimsiness, these leaps destined like those of an illusionist to baffle and impress.[19]

To make an assessment of the receptivity of his audience was nothing new to Le Corbusier, who formed calculated decisions about such things on a constant basis. If, as I will argue, there are links between Le Corbusier's rhetoric, and the structure of the promenade it follows that the promenade, expressed in what he called "solid words",[20] was choreographed to make sense to a particular audience, or to make sense at a variety of different levels.

Evidence of this rhetorical structure in Le Corbusier's written work can be found in *When the Cathedrals were White*, dating from roughly the same period that he evolved his ideas on rhetoric. Here the first section "Atmospheres" is designed to "open a window" to allow you to "breathe the exhausting atmosphere in which we are struggling". It is intentionally disorientating. "Rather than a narrative" these pages form "the consid-

---

16   See Tim Benton, *Le Corbusier conférencier*, p.26 for a further discussion of this issue.
17   Ibid., pp.26–27.
18   Ibid., p.37.
19   Le Corbusier, *Precisions* (Cambridge MA: MIT, 1991). Originally published as *Précisions sur un état présent de l'architecture et de l'urbanisme* (Paris: Crès, 1930), p.20.
20   "Ou en est l'architecture?", p.192.

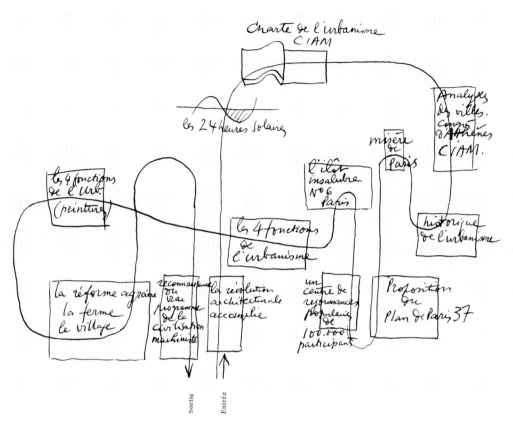

3.5 **The route through the Pavillon des Temps Nouveaux (1937) from the _Œuvre Complète_.**

ered reaction of a man lifted up by hope for times of strength and harmony".[21] Le Corbusier then moves on to clarify the problem before suggesting a solution, based of course upon his own œuvre. This does not mean that all his books conform to this pattern, _Towards a New Architecture_, for example, has a mystifying structure, probably as a result of its origins in the journal _L'Esprit Nouveau_. _Une Maison – un Palais_ is similarly disorganised also, I would suggest, because of the circumstances in which it was written.[22]

It is my thesis that ideas about rhetoric affected the design of routes through Le Corbusier's buildings. The Pavillon des Temps Nouveaux was itself structured around a "tribune for orators",[23] exhibition and oration being two forms of the same thing in Le Corbusier's mind (Fig. 3.4). A plan made for the route through the exhibition provides a particularly telling example (Fig. 3.5).[24] Upon entry the visitor was flattered by a section on "the architectural revolution accomplished". This led directly on to one of Le Corbusier's mysterious signs, that of the 24-hour day at the heart of the space and a barrage of CIAM information on the achievements of the past, all mildly confusing. Having been softened up in this way the visitor was thrown into the shock section "Misery of Paris". This was followed by a selection of exemplars from Le Corbusier's work, leading inevitably to a series of recommendations for the future. The visitor is in this way exposed to the full force of Le Corbusier's rhetoric, this time in built form.

21 Le Corbusier, _When the Cathedrals were White_ (New York: Reynal and Hitchcock, 1947), p.xxii. Originally published as _Quand les cathédrales étaient blanches_ (Paris: Plon, 1937).

22 Le Corbusier, _Une Maison – un palais. A la recherche d'une unité architecturale_ (Paris: Crès, 1928), pp.68–79.

23 Le Corbusier and Pierre Jeanneret, _Œuvre Complète Volume 3_, p.166.

24 Ibid., p.164.

Although Le Corbusier's interest in classical civilisation would have led him directly to a reading of key philosophers such as Aristotle, it is possible that he became familiar with the rules of rhetoric via his interest in film and narrative. Gustav Freytag in his 1863 book *Technique of Drama* – strongly influenced by Aristotle – linked the rhetorical stages with what he described as the basic stages of a unified drama, now known as Freytag's five-part dramatic arc or Freytag's triangle, used by film makers and others as a means to structure narrative.[25] These consist of:

a.   Introduction (exposition)
b.   Rise (development)
c.   Climax
d.   Return or fall (resolution)
e.   Catastrophe (denouement)

They describe a build-up of tension, excitement and understanding. The terminology needs slight adjustment to lend itself to the structure of Le Corbusier's rhetoric described above, but there are clear links between them. My suggestion is, that what I have called "Le Corbusier's narrative path" can be described as follows:

a.   Introduction (threshold)
b.   Disorientation (sensitising)
c.   Questioning (*savoir habiter*)
d.   Reorientation
e.   Culmination (ecstatic union)

This last term, ecstatic union, might seem a little over the top for the completion of a drama or route, but I can find no term better able to convey the absolute state of liberation that Le Corbusier ultimately had in mind. Freytag's dramatic arc is often expressed diagrammatically as a triangle or a pyramid, a closed form showing a unified narrative. If Le Corbusier's narrative path was to be portrayed graphically, like his vision of evolution, it is likely that it would take a spiral form returning the reader back to roughly where he or she began, but at a slightly higher level.

I am not suggesting that Le Corbusier made explicit reference to Freytag or to the stages of Aristotle's rhetoric in the making of the promenade. What I am suggesting however is that Le Corbusier thought very carefully about the structuring of arguments and of space and that the routes through his buildings may be seen to conform to the five-part structure, further that the narrative path described above provides a useful starting point for a discussion of the choreography of Le Corbusier's work and, possibly, the work of any architect.

25   Edward Branigan, *Narrative Comprehension and Film* (London: Routledge, 1992).

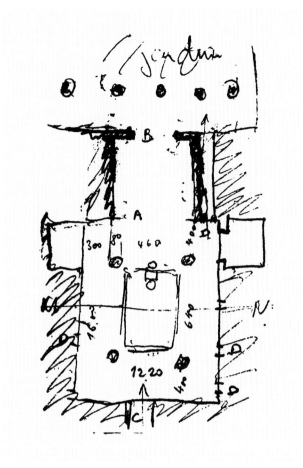

3.6 **The Casa del Noce, Pompeii from *Towards a New Architecture* (1923).**

Whilst on his travels as a young man, Le Corbusier described the experience of entry into the Casa del Noce in Pompeii[26] (Fig. 3.6):

Again the little vestibule which frees your mind from the street. And then you are in the Atrium; four columns in the middle (four cylinders) shoot up towards the shade of the roof, giving a feeling of force and a witness of potent methods; but at the far end is the brilliance of the garden seen through the peristyle which spreads out this light with a large gesture, distributes it and accentuates it, stretching widely from left to right, making a great space.[27]

The use of "again" at the start of the sentence suggests the presence of a pattern that Le Corbusier has noted repeatedly. As in the narrative path there are five stages to this sequence. Firstly the door which he omits to mention, but which receives extensive treatment elsewhere in his writings. Secondly the "vestibule" (c in Le Corbusier's plan) which, as Jan Birksted states, helps to "construct a particular state of mind, a state of receptivity".[28] In the third stage the reader becomes a "witness of potent methods", a passive experience in which he or she is exposed to a range of information. The fourth stage "the brilliance of the garden seen through the peristyle" is one of reorientation, the discovery of the path. The fifth stage is the attainment of that distant view, the climax of the journey.

26   An examination of a series of "croquis de voyages et etudes" that prefaces the *Œuvre Complete, Volume 1* shows an increasing interest in the promenade. Le Corbusier and Pierre Jeanneret, *Œuvre Complète Volume 1*, pp.17–21.

27   Le Corbusier, *Towards a New Architecture* (London: Architectural Press, 1982), p.169. Originally published as *Vers une Architecture* (Paris: Crès, 1923).

28   Jan Birksted, *Le Corbusier and the Occult* (Cambridge MA: MIT, 2009), p.160.

Le Corbusier's description of the experience of the Green Mosque in Broussa in the chapter the "Illusion of Plans" in *Towards a New Architecture* is similarly structured.

In Broussa in Asia Minor, at the Green Mosque, you enter by a little doorway of normal human height; a quite small vestibule produces in you the necessary change of scale so that you may appreciate, as against the dimensions of the street and the spot you come from, the dimensions with which it is intended to impress you. Then you can feel the noble size of the Mosque and your eyes can take its measure. You are in a great white marble space filled with light. Beyond you can see a second similar space of the same dimensions, but in half-light and raised on several steps (repetition in a minor key); on each side a still smaller space in subdued light; turning round, you have two very small spaces in shade. From full light to shade, a rhythm. Tiny doors and enormous bays. You are captured, you have lost the sense of the common scale. You are enthralled by a sensorial rhythm (light and volume) and by an able use of scale and measure, into a world of its own which tells you what it set out to tell you. What emotion, what faith! There you have motive and intention. The cluster of ideas, this is the means that has been used. In consequence, at Broussa as at Santa Sophia, as at the Suleiman Mosque of Stamboul, the exterior results from the interior.[29]

Here Le Corbusier describes a "cluster of ideas" available to those interested in the creation of routes. Firstly a change of scale helps you to appreciate the dimensions of the spaces around you, a technique used frequently in the sensitising or vestibule space of Le Corbusier's buildings. Secondly, whilst standing in a hall of particular dimension it is possible to see another hall of similar scale but in dim light, a "minor", slightly plaintive version of the space that you are in. Thirdly rhythms can be created with light and shade, emphasised through the contrasting use of tiny doors against large bays. In this way you "have lost the sense of common scale" heightening your sensitivity to issues of space. This careful build-up of drama reflects once more the structure of the narrative path.

Montage

One of the techniques used by Le Corbusier to bring together a range of diverse elements into a unified sequence is montage. Eisenstein refers to the montage sequence in terms of a path and it is here that we find its significance for the development of the promenade.

The word path is not used by chance. Nowadays it is the imaginary path followed by the eye and the varying perceptions of an object that depend on how it appears to the eye. Nowadays it may also be the path followed by the mind across a multiplicity of phenomena, far apart in time and space, gathered in a certain sequence into a single meaningful concept.[30]

Put very simply montage is about bringing together sequentially disparate images that cause the reader to make new associations between them. Elements of montage viewed in isolation are "dumb", but when seen together they spring into life.[31] The ultimate aim would be creation of a "completely balanced whole"[32] such as Auguste Choisy's plan of the Parthenon (Fig. 2.2) which Eisenstein believed to be "the perfect example of one of the most ancient films".[33] Indeed he described the route through the Acropolis in terms of "shots". For example:

29   Le Corbusier, *Towards a New Architecture*, pp.167–169.
30   Sergei Eisenstein, "Montage and Architecture" (c.1937), *Assemblage*, 10 (1989), p.116.
31   Ibid., p.128.
32   Ibid., p.118.
33   Ibid., p.117.

Shots a and b are equal in symmetry and, at the same time, the opposites of each other in spatial extent. Shots c and d are in mirror symmetry, and function, as it were, as enlargements of the right-hand and left-hand wings of shot a, then reforming again into a single balanced mass.[34]

It is not really necessary here to see what Eisenstein is referring to, what is important is to understand the games of affinity being played across the shots. Shot a and shot b are equal but opposite so the mind can make connections between them and so on. Other connective techniques are tonal coincidence – whereby the tones of two shots are similar – and rhythmic pattern – for example an oblique view of vertical railings being followed on by a horizontal set of steps. Obviously there are myriad techniques that editors use to link sequences of film together.[35] I highlight this issue here as it will play some part in the second part of this book when I try to break the promenade down into its constituent stages.

Le Corbusier's interest in montage is clearly expressed in his own "film" sequences which were made up of a sequence of stills. These developed, as Tim Benton records, out of the slide performances that accompanied his lectures in the 1920s which often took the form of hundreds of slides shown in quick succession. In 1924 he explained his use of "film" thus:

I arranged for the Sorbonne a sequence of slide projections whose purpose was to put the audience into a state of mental shock. Shock derived from a precipitate succession of heterogenous images – things from the past, from the present, contrasted and juxtaposed, sometimes also in harmony. Unexpected, dramatic relationships which in truth simply represented in visual form the state of the world today. Discordant relationships because we are in a discordant world, cutting ourselves off from tradition, a world giving birth in pain and contortion.[36]

This technique would receive extreme form in the performance of *Le Poème Electronique* (1958), introduced in chapter 1. Like Le Corbusier's other exhibitions it is a piece of polemic. It begins with the bull, the woman, the sun and other favoured elements of his symbolic repertoire in an odd, often disorientating juxta-position with Darwinian associations. These build up to the atrocities of Belsen (itself founded on ideas of natural selection) and war which is bound up with technology which jumps to a sequence of religious images which build up to Hiroshima. The last sequence is much more positive, Le Corbusier's manifesto for a happy future.

Transcending Time

Another technique of grouping that impacted upon Le Corbusier's work was that of the Surrealists who advocated chance as a means of creating order between disparate things. Le Corbusier did not believe that the works of Surrealism were the arbitrary products of the subconscious that their creators claimed them to be. In his opinion they were "very clearly dependent of the products of straightforward conscious effort, sustained and logical, cross-checked by the necessary mathematics and geometry".[37] In other words, the symbolic language of Surrealism was learnt and it had order.

---

34   Ibid., pp.120–121.
35   See for example S.D, Katz, *Film Directing Shot by Shot* (Los Angeles: Michael Wiese Productions, 1991). K. Reisz and G. Millar, *The Technique of Film Editing* (Boston & Oxford: Communication Arts Books/Hastings House/Focal Press, 1968). D. Arijon, *Grammar of the Film Language* (Los Angeles: Silman-James Press, 1976).
36   Fondation Le Corbusier (hereafter referred to as FLC) C3 (8) 70, document entitled "Bâle 4". Translated in Tim Benton, *The Rhetoric of Modernism*, pp.67–68.
37   Le Corbusier, *The Decorative Art of Today*, p.187.

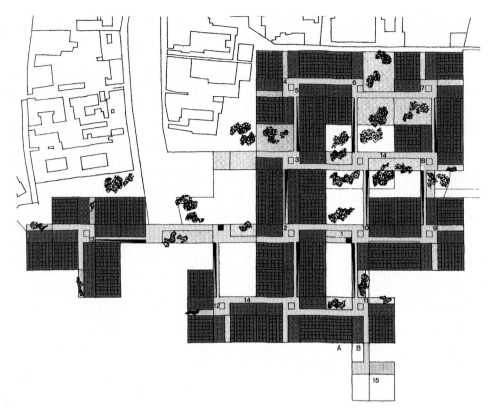

3.7 **Plan of the Venice Hospital (1966).**

Le Corbusier had a brief flirtation with Surrealism at the beginning of his career and was to remain friends, if distant, with André Breton (1896–1966), the self-styled leader of the Surrealists, for the rest of his life. To this end the presence of a copy of Breton's *L'Art magique* of 1957 in Le Corbusier's personal library in the FLC should be noted.[38] The Surrealist walks around Paris have now entered legendary status. Wandering around in a heightened state of sensitivity Breton and his friends would be delighted and amazed by odd incidents and curious collisions which would then be drawn back into their work.[39] Very late in his career Le Corbusier would use similar methods in the design process for the Venice Hospital (Fig. 3.7), one of the least hierarchical buildings that he ever designed. Here his long-term love affair with the city, the memories and events of a lifetime would be brought to play. Guillaume Jullian de Fuente who worked closely with Le Corbusier on the Venice Hospital reflected that:

… if you take small pieces of the hospital, you can relate them to Venice… The entire project was organised like that. All the circulation corridors and the halls… in the hospital were named after our own experiences of the city; the dead man, the knife, the cat, etc…, which corresponded to their resembling places of Venetian life. Thus this was not a problem of typology but poetry. In this poetic architectural approach, the mere fact "hospital" is almost incidental; it is integration to the life of the city that matters. And Le Corbusier discovered this essence of the city of Venice, its structure and its light – not the drawing board, but through his eyes his hands and even his feet, that is, by observing and going throughout it [the city] for a long time.[40]

38 It appears that Le Corbusier kept in contact with Breton on a sporadic basis for much of his life. For example there is a letter of 16 May 1949, FLC E109 216 from Breton to Le Corbusier. In one of his 1957 sketchbooks he noted to himself that he needed to get back in touch with Breton. Le Corbusier, *Sketchbooks Volume 3, 1954–1957* (Cambridge MA: MIT, 1982), sketch 959. It is Brassai – whose night time photos of Paris are used by Breton to illustrate his Surrealist walks – who photographs Le Corbusier writing in his apartment at 20 Rue Jacob in the late 1920s, one of a series of strong interconnections between the two men.

39 André Breton, *Mad Love* (Lincoln: University of Nebraska Press, 1987, pp.39–54. Originally published as *L'Amour Fou*, 1937.

40 P. Allard (2001), "Bridge over Venice: Speculations on Cross-fertilization of ideas between Team 10 and Le Corbusier (after a conversation with Guillaume Jullian de la Fuente)" in H. Sarkis (ed.) *CASE, Le Corbusier's Venice Hospital* (Munich: Prestel, 2001), p.30.

This is an extremely significant statement. Although the hospital is ostensibly a regular grid conforming largely to a mat typology it encompasses an internal travelogue of his experiences of the city of Venice.

Le Corbusier's late work is intensely picturesque. Jan Birksted believes that it is important to make a distinction between the picturesque – often associated with the eighteenth century English landscape garden – and the *pittoresque* which is, for Choisy, "an optical tableau that involves assymetrical volumes in an irregular landscape" and is something rather different.[41] Whilst the pittoresque might have come into play in Le Corbusier's early Purist work the latter buildings share in those flights of memory, imagination and movement that is so often associated with the picturesque, a word that he uses with no disdain.[42]

Both Breton and Le Corbusier shared a belief spawned by figures such as Apollinaire that the visionary poet had the ability to transcend time and to gain contact with the past that lay deep within his subconscious.[43] Only in this way could he become whole. Similarly montage was used by Eisenstein to juxtapose "phenomena, far apart in time and space".[44] Such ideas underpin Le Corbusier's obsession with bringing together objects and ideas from different times and situations that will be illustrated extensively in Part 2 of this book.

"There is nothing new under the sun: all things meet again across time and space, a proof of the oneness of human concerns which set men thinking, everywhere, up and down the scale".[45] "The Great Stories" like those of Theseus and the Minotaure, Dante and Beatrice, Jesus and Mary were never far from his mind, repeating across time and space.[46] As the novelist John McGahern writes in his own autobiography: "The story was still important, but I had read so many stories that I knew now that all true stories are essentially the laws of life in both its sameness and its endless variations."[47] Towards the end of his life Le Corbusier began to embed increments of his own memories and associations into his architecture believing them to be in some way archetypal. He wrote of his own weakness in wanting to see his ideas in grander terms. "I should prefer that my ideas had a consequence rather than being my exclusive and personal property."[48]

Orphic Initiation

The architectural promenade was conceived as a form of initiatory route into the powers of harmonious unity – "the mystery is not negligible, is not to be rejected, is not futile. It is the minute of silence in our toil. It awaits the initiate".[49] It is not surprising therefore that Charles Edouard Jeanneret (the young Le Corbusier) was

41   Jan Birksted, *Le Corbusier and the Occult* (Cambridge MA: MIT, 2009). p.85.
42   Le Corbusier and Pierre Jeanneret, *Œuvre Complète Volume 3, 1934–38* (Zurich: Les Editions Girsberger, 1945), p.168. Originally published in 1938.
43   V. Spate, *Orphism: the Evolution of Non-figurative Painting in Paris in 1910–14* (Oxford: Clarendon, 1979), p.62.
44   Sergei Eisenstein, "Montage and Architecture" (c.1937), *Assemblage* 10 (1989), p.116.
45   Le Corbusier, *Modulor 2* (London: Faber, 1955), p.33. Originally published as *Le Modulor II* (Paris: Editions d'Architecture d'Aujourd'hui, 1955).
46   Le Corbusier has much in common in this respect with Carl Jung. On the relationship between his ideas and those of Jung see Flora Samuel, "Animus, Anima and the Architecture of Le Corbusier", *Harvest*, 48, 2 (2003), pp.42–60.
47   J. McGahern, *Memoire* (London: Faber and Faber, 2006), p.241.
48   Letter to Ritter, 14.1.26, Paris, FLC R3-19-408. Quoted in Weber, N. F., *Le Corbusier: A Life* (New York: Knopf, 2008), p.228.
49   Le Corbusier, *The Decorative Art of Today*, p.181. Le Corbusier also told Trouin that an "initiation" was necessary to understand his art properly. Letter Trouin to Le Corbusier, 1945, FLC 13 01 9.

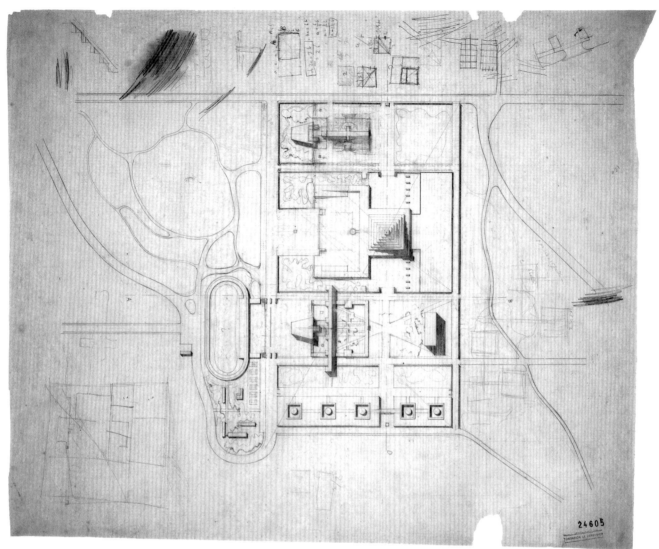

3.8 **Mundaneum scheme (1928), FLC 24605.**

3.9 **Le Corbusier by his bed at 24 Rue Nungesser et Coli in front of a painting by André Bauchant
depicting a horned god at once Dionysiac and Orphic.**

impressed by Edouard Schuré's book *Les Grands Initiés* at the core of which is a description of the life of
Orpheus and an initiation into the mysteries of the "radiant spirit" Dionysos[50] to discover "the secret of
worlds, the soul of nature and the essence of God".[51] Schuré's words made a very strong impression upon
Jeanneret who in January 1908 wrote excitedly to his parents that the book had "opened horizons" to him
which had "filled" him with "happiness".[52] The book was to provide the focus for his Mundaneum scheme
(1928), a square spiral route up and then down into a ziggurat at the base of which was a "sacrarium" filled
with the "Grands Initiés" that Schuré held so dear (Fig. 3.8).[53]

Having renounced the religion within which he was raised Jeanneret sought a form of belief, an ordering
system, that could link back to the past (Fig. 3.9). Hence the appeal of Orphism, based on the ancient mystery
religion of that name and built around the legend of Orpheus who, with his beautiful music, managed to
persuade the gods to allow him to visit the Underworld to rescue his lost love Euridice from Death. Orphism
simultaneously referred to an art movement instigated by Apollinaire which included Le Corbusier's friend
Fernand Léger amongst its proponents.[54] These artists took inspiration from Orpheus' ability to create harmony through his music, wanting to achieve a similar state of harmony through painting – by using colour
and form to affect the emotions.

50   Chapter entitled "Orphée (Le mystères de Dionysos)" in E. Schuré, *Les Grands Initiés: Esquisse secrète des religions* (Paris: Perrin, 1908), p.219 in FLC.
51   Ibid., p.232.
52   Letter Le Corbusier to his parents, 31.1.1908 in the archives at La Chaux de Fonds (CdF LCms 34, transcription supplied by Mlle Françoise Frey). Quoted
     by Benton, "The Sacred and the Search for Truths", in Tim Benton (ed.), *Le Corbusier: Architect of the Century* (London: Arts Council, 1987), p.239.
53   Translated from Le Corbusier and Jeanneret, *Œuvre Complète Volume 1*, p.190.
54   Virginia Spate, "Orphism", in Nikos Stangos (ed.), *Concepts of Modern Art* (London: Thames and Hudson, 1997), p.194.

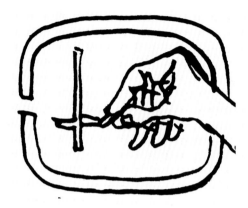

3.10 **"Tool" from *Le Poème de l'angle droit* (1955).**

Le Corbusier's profound interests in Pythagoreanism, Plato, Catharism, Cabalism, Neo-Platonism, alchemy, the troubadours, the medieval master builders and early Christianity are all, in essence, Orphic as they share a concern with asceticism, number, and balance – of light and dark (complete with Manichaean subtext), of spirit and body, of male and female, as well as a series of other oppositions, all of which receive expression through his architecture and are manifested in the promenade for those "with eyes to see".

The Alchemical Journey

That Le Corbusier took a profound interest in the stages of the ancient science of alchemy has been demonstrated by Richard A. Moore, Peter Carl, Mogen Krustrup and other commentators. The alchemical process took place in a series of transformations starting with base matter and finishing with the marriage of opposites, man and woman, symbolised by *sol* and *luna*, sun and moon. The transformation took place through the *coniunctio*, symbolised by their sexual union, which culminated in the attainment of the "philosopher's stone", sometimes expressed geometrically as "the squaring of the circle". The alchemical hermaphrodite became an important symbol of this process. "He who experiences this transformation has no more desires, and the prolongation of earthly life has no more importance for him who already lives in the deathless." The point that is most significant for the promenade is that experiments were conducted in the spiritual and material world simultaneously, these two realms remaining inextricably linked. The journey of the spirit had parallels in the material world.

The alchemical process is strongly implicated in *Le Poème de l'angle droit*. It has already been mentioned that Le Corbusier made the key, or contents page, of this book into what he called an iconostasis, a sequence of panels in the form of a tree (Fig. 2.22). Traditionally the iconostasis was linked to the icons of Christ and Mary.[55] Le Corbusier's own iconostasis appears to focus on Le Corbusier's own psychological transformation through his relationship with his wife Yvonne, one of the stories that is echoed in the promenade, particularly that of Ronchamp.[56]

---

55   Le Corbusier, *Journey to the East* (Cambridge MA: MIT, 1987), p.62. Originally published as *Le Voyage d'Orient* (Paris: Parenthèses, 1887).

56   See Flora Samuel, *Le Corbusier Architect and Feminist* (London: Wiley, 2004).

Numerical symbolism plays a role in this transformation. At the top of the tree there are five squares devoted to "milieu" corresponding to the five squares on the third level down which are devoted to the theme of "flesh". "Milieu" is a complex word expressive of nature in its raw, original sense. "Environment" is not an adequate translation of this term. Both "milieu" and "flesh" have five squares. According to Louis Réau, one of Le Corbusier's contemporaries, in Christian art the number five corresponds to the five senses,[57] an appropriate association if Le Corbusier was trying to emphasise the links between these layers and the body. The layer in between "milieu" and "flesh" – "spirit" – has three squares, corresponding, as Réau would have it, to the Trinity.[58] The top three layers of *Le Poème de l'angle* droit are thus devoted numerically to this most central concern of Le Corbusier, the relationship of spirit and matter.[59] Further, it cannot be accidental that the iconostasis has seven layers.[60] For Réau seven was a number which was "particularly august".[61] It could be obtained by adding three, symbolic of the Trinity, and four, symbolic of earthly concerns (such as the seasons and the elements). The number seven thus represented, amongst other things, the order of the universe, in other words, harmony.[62]

"Fusion" an image of the alchemical union of opposites "offering", an image of Le Corbusier's open hand and "tool", at the bottom of *Le Poème*, are each given one square (Fig. 3.10). All the layers of the iconostasis devoted specifically to the cause of unity, occupy a single square, the number one being, for the mediaeval builders, symbolic of unity and of God.[63] "Tool" shows Le Corbusier's hand holding a piece of carbon with which he draws the right angle in a thick black line.

The alchemical process took place in a series of stages each, like the layers of the iconostasis, associated with a particular colour. Colour was used within *Le Poème* to carry meaning as it was, for example, in the Pavillon des Temps Nouveaux something that is lost from view in its black and white photographic representations. Here the reader would enter through a blue wall to be faced with an opposing wall of an intense red, with green to the left and grey on the right, the floor throughout being of pale yellow gravel.[64] The green, grey and blue through which the visitor passes constitute a return to nature or rebirth. The yellow both underfoot and emanating as light through the glazed roof is always the masculine sun or spirit in Le Corbusier's work, the red that confronts the reader is the colour of fusion or physicality. Colour symbolism would create an extra level of meaning within the promenade – "you resort to using colour, to arrange things according to an order".[65] As in the work of the alchemists colour was used by Le Corbusier to emphasise his message in a manner both enigmatic and manipulative.

57   Louis Réau, *Iconographie de l'art Chrétien Volume 1* (Paris: Presses Universitaires de France, 1955), p.68.
58   The Trinity traditionally stands for Father, Son and Holy Ghost but was given rather different treatment in Le Corbusier's hands, referring I suggest to Mary and Mary Magdalene – associated with his wife Yvonne and his mother Marie in the chapels of Ronchamp. See Flora Samuel, "A Profane Annunciation. The Representation of Sexuality in the Architecture of Ronchamp", *Journal of Architectural Education*, 53, 2 (1999), pp.74–90.
59   According to Balkrishna Doshi Le Corbusier was very superstitious. Carmen Kagal, "Le Corbusier: the Acrobat of Architecture. Interview with Balkrishna Doshi, 1986", *Architecture and Urbanism*, 322 (1997), pp.168–183.
60   Ghyka wrote "In Pythagorean Number-Mystic, seven was the Virgin-Number". Matila Ghyka, *The Geometry of Art and Life* (New York: Dover, 1977), p.21. Originally published in 1946.
61   Réau, *Iconographie de l'art Chrétien Volume 1*, p.68.
62   See also Emile Mâle, *The Gothic Image* (London: Fontana, 1961), p.11. Originally published in 1910.
63   Réau, *Iconographie de l'art Chrétien Volume 1*, p.68.
64   Le Corbusier and Pierre Jeanneret, *Œuvre Complète Volume 3*, p.169.
65   Interview by Le Corbusier with Robert Mallet, 1951. Quoted in Caroline Maniaque, *Le Corbusier and the Maisons Jaoul*, p.25.

The Oracle of the Holy Bottle

Le Corbusier was fascinated by the journey to the Oracle of Holy Bottle set out by François Rabelais (c.1494–1553) in his book *Gargantua and Pantagruel* (1534), a play on the archetypal story of initiation. Confirming the importance of this author's ideas to his work, Le Corbusier wrote:

And it always ends with
This darned Rabelais – the builder, the right angle, the sain [as opposed to the saintly] the director of everything…
Rabelais he is the two co-ordinates; the horizontal and the vertical = what interests the body, the soul and the gut of man.[66]

It quickly becomes evident to anyone who reads through the four volumes of Le Corbusier's sketchbooks that Rabelais' book *Gargantua and Pantagruel*, introduced to him in his youth, occupied a very important place in the life of the architect – "good Pantagruel… The book… this book is always in my hand". On April 3, 1954, whilst working on the Chapel of Ronchamp, Le Corbusier started a new sketchbook, entitled H32. He copied into it, although not word for word, several pages of Book Five of *Gargantua and Pantagruel*, those pages in which Panurge seeks advice from the Oracle of the Holy Bottle on whether or not to marry.[67]

It is what Le Corbusier calls the "miraculandolous"[68] – Neoplatonist Pico della Mirandola (1463–1494) provides a strong clue as to what is going on here. He notes that it was the practice of ancient theologians to cover the mysteries of Orpheus' teachings "with the wrappings of fables, and disguise them with a poetic garment, so that whoever reads his hymns may believe that there is nothing underneath but tales and the purest nonsense".[69] According to Pico the Orphics had "a secret doctrine of number" that was understood and utilised by the ancient Egyptians, Pythagoras, Plato, Aristotle and Origen.[70] Significantly, in sketchbook H32, it is Le Corbusier's consideration of the issue of proportion and harmony both in music and in art that leads him directly on to Rabelais' description of Panurge's arrival at the sanctuary of the Holy Bottle and a complex analysis of the route in terms of number. Le Corbusier's transcription begins:

…arrived in the longed for isle…
At the end of this fatal number you will find the Temple door…
= true psychogony of Plato so celebrated by the
Academicians and so little understood, of which half is
composed of unity, the first two whole numbers, of two
squares and of two cubes (1 = 2 and 3 = squared 8 and 27 Total 54 = Plato
they descend 108 steps…[71]

The presence of these numbers fills Panurge with fear, such import do they carry. Scribbled calculations and notes next to his transcribed text suggest that Le Corbusier cogitated over the meaning of these figures for some time searching for their inner significance. Panurge is dressed in ritual clothing and is taken through

---

66   Le Corbusier, *Sketchbooks Volume 3*, sketches 645–646.
67   Ibid. sketches 85–88. For an expansion of this discussion see Flora Samuel, "Le Corbusier, Rabelais and the Oracle of the Holy Bottle", *Word and Image*, 16 (2000), pp.1–13.
68   Le Corbusier, *Sketchbooks Volume 3*, sketch 1011.
69   Pico della Mirandola, *On the Dignity of Man* (Indianapolis: Hackett, 1998), p.33.
70   Ibid., p. 30–31.
71   Le Corbusier, *Sketchbooks Volume 3*, p.10.

the process of initiation into the mysteries of the Holy Bottle, all of this described in ornate detail. He arrives at the innermost sanctuary where, after all this anticipation, the word "trink" emanates from the oracle itself, perhaps one of the greatest anticlimaxes in literary history. Despite this Le Corbusier respond with excitement: "To assist my own understanding, I interpret: act, and you shall see the miracle. Do not seek a gloss! Do not try to escape! The bottle tells you: Drink."[72] Clearly he took this comic journey of initiation very seriously indeed.

La Sainte Baume

Le Corbusier's scheme for a Basilica, housing, museum and park at La Sainte Baume in Provence (1945–1960) was to be built around the archetypal journey from darkness to light, embodied in the stories of Orpheus and Rabelais. Indeed it was designed as an initiatory route into the harmonious delights of Orphism. If built it would have provided a synthesis of many of the ordering techniques described in this chapter. We know this because Le Corbusier's client for the scheme Edouard Trouin was extremely indiscreet in his letters to the architect causing Le Corbusier to admonish him with a warning to take great care with what he put in writing, but never refuting what was said.[73] That Le Corbusier concurred with Trouin's ideas can be deduced from his letters of his support, the longevity of their association and from his own determination to advance the project when Trouin had all but given up on it. Further, describing it as "an astonishing and perhaps marvellous undertaking", he gave the scheme great prominence in the pages of his *Œuvre Complète*.[74]

La Sainte Baume was for Trouin "the philosophical city"

City   – of Rabelais   Orphic[75]
      – of Saint Teresa[76]

The relationship between the intiatory route of the Basilica and the ideas of Rabelais has already been alluded to in the discussion of the Oracle of the Holy Bottle, but the role of St Teresa is also significant here. Rabelais' volume *Gargantua and Pantagruel* was published in 1534. St Teresa's works were roughly contemporary, *The Way of Perfection*[77] being finished in 1567 and *The Interior Castle*[78] being written approximately ten years later. Rabelais and St Teresa occupied the hinge of history between the medieval period and the Renaissance, an age of great tension between orthodox Catholicism and other more esoteric versions of Christianity, a time when accusations of heresy were rife meaning it became necessary to communicate unorthodox ideas in symbol and allusion. In *The Interior Castle*, based upon the idea of a chivalric quest, the

---

72   Ibid., p.210.
73   "Take care, for the love of God!" Letter Le Corbusier to Trouin, 7 March 1956, FLC 13 01 106.
74   Le Corbusier, *Œuvre Complète Volume 5*, 1946–1952 (Zurich: Les Editions d'Architecture, 1973), pp.24–28. Originally published in 1953.
75   Trouin, "Table provisoire" for book entitled "La Sainte Baume et Marie Madeleine," n.d., FLC 13 01 399.
76   Flora Samuel, "The Philosophical City of Rabelais and St Teresa. Le Corbusier and Edouard Trouin's scheme for St Baume", *Literature and Theology*, 13, 2 (1999), pp.111–126.
77   St Teresa of Jesus, *The Way of Perfection* (London: Thomas Baker, 1911).
78   St Teresa of Jesus, *The Interior Castle* (London: Thomas Baker, 1912), originally written in 1577.

3.11 **Chapel of Mary Magdalene built into the side of the escarpment at La Sainte Baume.**

3.12 **Pilgrimage route up to the Mary Magdalene's grotto at La Sainte Baume.**

pilgrim passes along a crystalline route into the complex recesses of the soul. It was necessary to pass through one stage of understanding before moving on to the next. This idea of spiritual space within the confines of the body is one that I will refer to in later chapters.

La Sainte Baume is the site of the grotto of Mary Magdalene set high up in the side of the cliff face overlooking a wide flat valley (Fig. 3.11). She is significant to this account as, being what Trouin called the "prostitute saint", she exemplified the process by which knowledge of the body could lead to spiritual understanding, an idea that is fundamental to Le Corbusier's work and to the promenade.[79]

Magdalene is also connected to geometry as it is said that she brought a knowledge of number to France from the East to live as a hermit in the grotto at La Sainte Baume, sustained only by the songs of angels who carried her up to the top of the cliff each day (Fig. 3.12).[80] The promenade of the basilica is an echo of her story, a descent into confusion, darkness and sensory excess to be followed by clarity, geometry and light.

La Sainte Baume was a particularly august place of pilgrimage for the Masonic group of the *Compagnons du Tour de France* who saw themselves as the direct descendents of the early master craftsmen. As part of

For further evidence see Flora Samuel, "Le Corbusier, Teilhard de Chardin and La Planétisation humaine: spiritual ideas at the heart of modernism", *French Cultural Studies,* 11, 2 (2000), pp.181–200.
80 This is the Provençal version of her story. See Flora Samuel, *Orphism in the Work of Le Corbusier, La Sainte Baume 1945–1960*, unpublished PhD thesis, Cardiff (2000), pp.95–100.

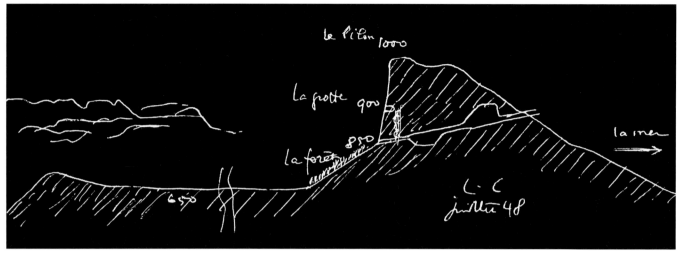

3.13 **Le Corbusier's scheme for the Basilica at La Sainte Baume (1948) from the *Œuvre Complète*.**

their process of initiation they made a tour of France to a series of sites of great significance to the order, La Sainte Baume being one of them.[81] Antoine Moles, their leader, who was well acquainted with Le Corbusier,[82] believed that they had inherited from their medieval forebears a secret knowledge of number and proportion. It is therefore very significant that crypts for this order were to be provided within the confines of Trouin and Le Corbusier's scheme.[83]

The documentation makes clear that the Basilica was conceived as a route of initiation with origins in very early religion, particularly the processional routes of ancient Egypt.[84] Inspiration also came from "the Parthenon, the Indian temples, and the cathedrals which were all built according to precise measures which constituted a code, a coherent system: a system which proclaimed essential unity".[85]

Le Corbusier's Basilica can be seen in his sketch of July 1948 (Fig. 3.13).[86] In the form of a route, his scheme resembled in cross section a drawn out mandala, a representation of the cyclical form of the cosmos, derived from his symbol of the 24-hour day, already discussed in chapter 1 (Fig. 1.5), which he described as the summary of all his efforts.

If meditation upon this figure could produce striking results in the susceptible, then the best way to facilitate the journey to the "Lost Paradise", the original unity at the end of the Orphic journey, would be to place the initiate actually within the sign itself to experience its power at first hand. In Mircea Eliade's words: "Penetration into a mandala drawn on the ground is equivalent to an initiation ritual... the mandala protects the neophyte against every harmful force from without, and at the same time helps him to concentrate, to find his own 'centre'."[87]

---

81   Jan Birksted, *Le Corbusier and the Occult*, p.247.

82   See inscription to Le Corbusier in A. Moles, *Histoire des Charpentiers* (Paris: Librairie Gründ, 1949) in FLC.

83   Edouard Trouin (Louis Montalte pseud.), *Le Basilique Universelle de la Paix et du Pardon*, FLC 13 01 403. Antonin Raymond, *An Autobiography* (Vermont: Charles E. Tuttle Company, 1973), p.150.

84   Trouin, "Plan D'Aups ou Plan-Plan D'Aups", n.d., FLC 13 01 369. Le Corbusier was finally to visit Egypt in 1952 when he made a highly detailed sketch of "the sacred processional route of Chephren" amongst other things, involving many measurements and numerical calculations. Le Corbusier, *Sketchbooks Volume 2, 1950–54* (London: Thames and Hudson, 1981), sketch 773.

85   Le Corbusier, *The Modulor* (London: Faber, 1951), p.18. Originally published as *Le Modulor* (Paris: Editions de l'Architecture d'aujourd'hui, 1950), p.18.

86   There were three versions of the Basilica scheme. The first produced by Trouin in 1946, the version by Le Corbusier described here and a final version the "Vallon du Béton" designed by the two men together.

87   Mircea Eliade, *Images and Symbols* (London: Harville Press, 1961), p.53.

At La Sainte Baume the initiate would be drawn into the Basilica, a symbol deriving from dark and light, night and day, body and spirit, the most basic dualisms of Manichaen religion. He or she would experience the Basilica as, what he called "a remarkable, invisible architectural undertaking with an enormous effort dedicated to the interior, aimed solely at moving those souls which are capable of understanding".[88]

If Le Corbusier's narrative path is applied to the scheme for La Sainte Baume, the first stage of the promenade begins at the start of the pilgrimage wherever it may be. The second disorientation stage would occur on entry into the mountain. Stage three would be what Le Corbusier called a "descent to the sources of sensation"[89] into the lower segment of the Basilica, the third questioning phase of the narrative. The implication here is that the body would give access to enlightenment, in other words reorientation which occurs in the fourth stage in the narrative.[90] This is the point at which the neophyte rejoins the route up and out of the mountain. Le Corbusier carefully sited the fifth stage of the narrative path at a point where the descending slope of the mountain St Pilon crossed the ascending slope of the Pitou beyond it.[91]

Inside, the rock would be an example of the work of architecture, movement, natural diurnal lighting, artificial lighting on one side of the rock from the entrance to the Saint Magdalene Grotto to the other side, suddenly opening on to the striking light of a never-ending horizon, towards the sea in the south.[92]

This would be the culmination of the journey.

Conclusion

This chapter has focussed on the systems of order used by Le Corbusier to give structure to his arguments and make sense of this chaotic world. Whilst the stages of what I have called Le Corbusier's narrative path, described above, have their origins in Aristotle and Freytag's understanding of rhetoric and drama, they are echoed in the initiatory stories of Orpheus, Mary Magdalene, Panurge and Theseus (whose journey to the labyrinth was discussed in chapter 3) and the story of Jacob (which plays an important role in chapter 5). They share a common narrative, a descent into the underworld of confusion and darkness followed by transformation, revelation, enlightenment and peace, a sequence of events that Le Corbusier seems to have identified with at a very personal level, one that has much in common with what the analytical psychologist C.G. Jung called the process of individuation.[93]

---

88   Le Corbusier, *Œuvre Complète Volume 5*, p.25.
89   Le Corbusier, *Sketchbooks Volume 2*, sketch 799.
90   These suppositions are backed up extensively in Flora Samuel, *La Sainte Baume 1945–1960: Orphism in the Work of Le Corbusier*.
91   Le Corbusier, *Œuvre Complète Volume 5*, p.27.
92   Ibid., p.25.
93   Flora Samuel, "Animus, Anima and the Architecture of Le Corbusier", pp.42–60.

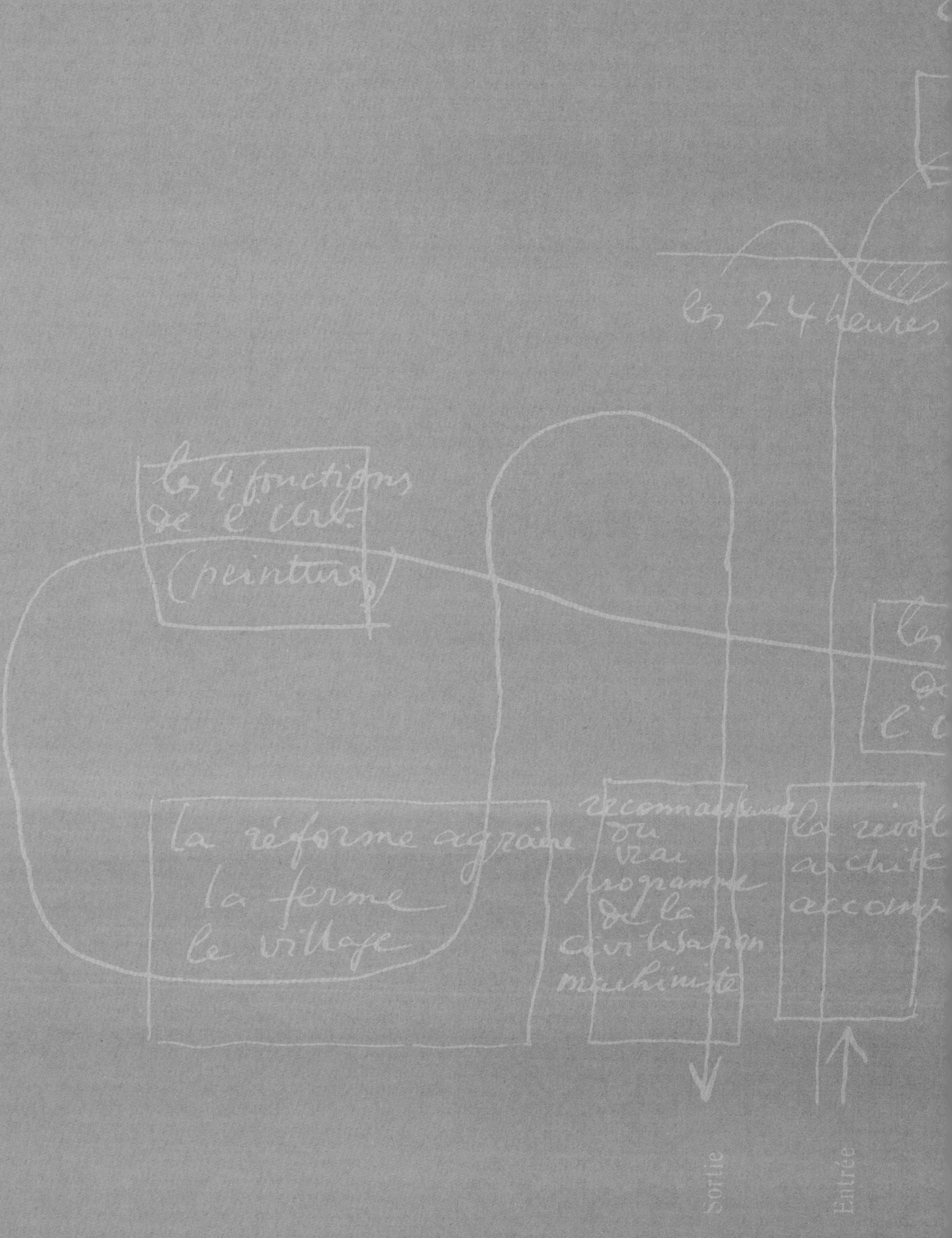

les 24 heures

les 4 fonctions
de l'Urb.
(peinture)

la réforme agraire
la ferme
le village

reconnaissance
du vrai
programme
de la
civilisation
machiniste

la révol
archite
accomp

les
de
l'a

Sortie

Entrée

Part 2 – Solid Words: The Rhetoric of Architecture

4.1 **Stair up to the pulpit of Notre-Dame du Haut, Ronchamp (1955).**

4. Elements of the Architectural Promenade

Drawing from the first part of the book it is possible to arrive at a hypothesis about what the promenade might be, a series of unfolding views following a series of different axes, beginning in darkness and ending in light. Mathematical proportion and relationships would reinforce the effect. Further film technique would be implicated in the unfolding of views. Overlapping frames derived from Le Corbusier's experiments in art would create tension between foreground and background, causing space to fluctuate, one moment one thing, another moment different, urging us on. Ultimately the promenade would constitute a series of experiences of space, texture, light, memories, associations or things that would be stitched together into an initiation into the pleasures of *savoir habiter*. This second part of the book will illustrate how this panoply of persuasive techniques manifested themselves in his architecture, in doing so revealing a genealogy in the development of the promenade.

In *Towards a New Architecture* Le Corbusier called for "a minute study of every detail connected with the house, and a close search for a standard, that is for a type".[1] The type detail would be the best detail possible for that particular material or situation. *Le Corbusier and the Architectural Promenade* follows on in logical progression from my earlier book *Le Corbusier in Detail* which set out the basic categories of type detail used and reused by Le Corbusier across his career and the motivations behind them. The aim of this chapter is to document the elements which typically make up each stage in Le Corbusier's narrative path.

Threshold or Introduction

The threshold into the domain of Le Corbusier, often muted in its lighting, provides a point of focus after the "mental silence of the street".[2] In many instances it occurs at some distance from the building itself or will itself have a number of incremental elements strung out along the route building up to the point of entry.

Le Corbusier fully recognised the important function of doors and thresholds in linking disparate realms, each one for him being a "gateway of reverie"[3] (Fig. 4.2). The door, the mat well, the handle, the awning, the floor finishes, the articulation of ceiling and threshold – all these play a critical role in the formulation of entry. The door marks the point of transition between two realities, expressed in these words from *Le Poème de l'angle droit*.

It is through the doors of
open eyes that looks
exchanged have led to
the flash of communion[4]

---

1   Le Corbusier, *Towards a New Architecture* (London: Architectural Press, 1982), p.246. Originally published as *Vers une Architecture* (Paris: Crès, 1923).

2   Le Corbusier and Pierre Jeanneret *Œuvre Complète Volume 1*, 1910–1929 (Zurich: Girsberger, 1943), p.52. Originally published in 1937.

3   Le Corbusier, *Journey to the East* (Cambridge MA: MIT, 1987), p.70. Originally published as *Le Voyage d'Orient* (Paris: Parenthèses, 1887).

4   Le Corbusier, *Le Poème de l'angle droit* (Paris: Editions Connivance, 1989), Section D.3, Fusion. Originally published in 1955.

4.2 **Door from *Le Poème de l'angle droit* (1955).**

Doors and eyes are almost interchangeable. The building, as in the films of Eisenstein, is a protagonist in the drama, entering into a tense and passionate relationship with the reader. At the Maison des Jeunes at Firminy the reader places his or her hand within the handprint of the building's door in a pact of solidarity and welcome (Fig. 4.3).

Always keen to emphasise the different types of "architectural sensation" afforded by doors, Le Corbusier wrote:

To the young student, I should ask: How do you make a door? What size?
Where do you put it? … I want reasons for that. And I should add: Hold on: do you open a door? Why there and not elsewhere? Ah, you seem to have many solutions? You are right, there are many possible solutions and each gives a different architectural sensation. Ah, you realize that different solutions are the very basis of architecture? Depending on the way you enter a room, that is to say depending on the place of the door in the wall of the room, the feeling will be different. That is architecture![5]

The design of the entrance space itself does, of course, impact upon the reading of the door's importance. Even in the earliest houses, where the doors themselves are very understated, for example at the Maison La Roche, the act of entry through, even a secondary door,[6] is celebrated through the careful choreography of doormat and canopy (Fig. 4.4), cantilevered at an angle to welcome visitors or, as at the Villa at Vaucresson (1922) protected by a balcony.

The pivoting door is perhaps the most distinctive of Corbusian doors as it has such a radical effect upon the space in which it sits. It is often made of the same material as the space itself meaning that, when closed,

5   Le Corbusier, *Precisions* (Cambridge MA: MIT, 1991), p.73. Originally published as *Précisions sur un état présent de l'architecture et de l'urbanisme* (Paris: Crès, 1930).
6   Fondation Le Corbusier (hereafter referred to as FLC) 15125, H. Allen Brookes (ed.), *The Le Corbusier, Archive, Volume I* (New York: Garland, 1983), p.489. Hereafter referred to as Allen Brookes, *Archive I*.

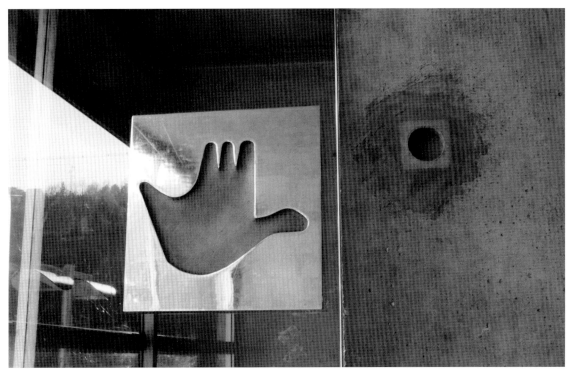

4.3 **Door handle Maison des Jeunes (1965).**

4.4 **Secondary door Maison La Roche (1923).**

4.5 Piero della Francesca (1410/1420–1492), *The Flagellation* (1447). Panel held at the National Gallery of Le Marche, in the Palazzo Ducale, Urbino, CAL-F-008159-0000. Reproduced with the permission of Ministero per i Beni e le Attività Culturali.

it feels as though it barely exists. "Just realize the *architectural fact* of this little door set into the wall. The other architectural fact of the door is cutting the wall in two."[7] This longitudinal division of space is reflected in Le Corbusier's doors which often have two very different faces such as that into the living room of the penthouse at 24 Rue Nungesset et Coli to be discussed in chapter 6.

Pivoting doors became particularly prevalent in Le Corbusier's work – partly I would suggest – because of the symbolic possibilities inherent within them and partly because, when open, they encourage a feeling of spatial flow. So pleased was Le Corbusier with the design of the pivoting door for the Temps Nouveau exhibition that he included photographs of it both shut and open in the *Œuvre Complète* (Fig. 3.2).[8] The pivot of the door of 24 Rue Nungesser et Coli is not central, presumably to prevent it from obstructing the route too greatly. However, at the Heidi Weber Haus in Zurich, the pivots do occur at the midpoint of the door allowing traffic through in either direction.

The pivoting door invites a bisected view and a rather special view of space, like that in the paintings of Piero della Francesca, much loved by Le Corbusier (whose knowledge of art history was profound).[9] The structure of such paintings as the *Flagellation* (1447), or the *Annunciation* (1452) – encompassing contrasting views both near and far (Fig. 4.5) – is often repeated in his ordering of space. Thomas Schumacher writes:

… the genre [of the annunciation]… almost invariably uses a split screen; the angel is on the left and the Virgin is on the right. And while the figures of these compositions consistently oppose each other, creating a binary tension, the frame often holds the same tension. Left/right, inside and outside, then/now, near/far, all are in opposition, expressing the hinge of History that Christian doctrine attaches to this event.[10]

Le Corbusier used this format so frequently in his architecture and its representation that it is likely that it held some kind of significance for him. Often one side of the frame is dark, the other light, creating a tension between the physical world of the present and the spiritual world of the future.

Sometimes there is a door: one opens it – enters – one is in another realm, the realm of the gods, the room which holds the key to the great systems. These doors are the doors of the miracles. Having gone through one, man is no longer the operative force, but rather is his contact with the universe. In front of him unfolds and spreads out the fabulous fabric of numbers without end. He is in the country of numbers. He may be a modest man and yet have entered just the same. Let him remain, entranced by so much dazzling all-pervading light.[11]

The door is consistently a site of transformation and revelation.

The chapel at Ronchamp is a play upon transition and threshold. The enamel, bronze and cast iron processional door (2770 mm by 2770 mm), is itself set within a frame within a glazed frame (Fig. 4.6).[12] The exterior and interior finishes are continuous so the ceremonial door asserts its presence as threshold whilst, perhaps

7   Le Corbusier, *Precisions*, p.228.

8   Le Corbusier and Pierre Jeanneret, *Œuvre Complète Volume 3*, 1934–38 (Zurich: Les Editions Girsberger, 1945), p.162–163. Originally published in 1938.

9   See Stephen Kite, *An Architectonic Eye* (Oxford: Legenda, 2009), pp.142–143 for a discussion of "Piero and Perspective" much of which brings Le Corbusier strongly to mind.

10   T. Schumacher, "Deep Space Shallow Space". *Architectural Review*, vol. CLXXXI, no 1079 (1987), pp.37–43.

11   Le Corbusier, *Modulor 2* (London: Faber, 1955), p.71. Originally published as *Le Modulor II* (Paris: Editions d'Architecture d'Aujourd'hui, 1955).

12   Le Corbusier, *The Chapel at Ronchamp* (London: Architectural Press, 1957), p.107.

paradoxically, allowing the flow of space from outside in. A mat well appears to one side of the door indicating which side is for entry and which is for exit. A gap between the door and the walls of the building prevents the door from brutally bisecting its sweeping masonry curves whilst, in strong light, providing it with a shimmering halo (Fig. 4.7).

Anything but self-effacing, the Ronchamp door announces itself in a variety of ways: through the extreme contrast between its colourful shiny enamel surfaces and the surrounding walls; through its size; through the way that it is set deep within the monumental wall; through the presence of its independent frame; through its dramatic and large handle; through the smooth panel of stone set into the floor beneath it and through the choreography of the elements around it, the holy water stoop and so on. It is decorated with symbols which form the subject of an entire book by Mogens Krustrup.[13] The enamel door of the assembly at Chandigarh is similarly loaded with what Vikramaditya Prakash describes as an "Edenic subtext".[14] What seems so significant is the fact that Le Corbusier chose to adorn these highly important doors at Ronchamp in this way, the practice of ornamenting doors with magical talismans being ancient in the extreme. What better way to apprise the neophyte on the initiatory architectural promenade of the meaning of the quest?[15]

Sensitising Vestibule

The corollary of the door is the vestibule space, sometimes consisting of as little as a change in ceiling level or floor finish, but often taking the form of a lobby, vestibule or hall. I think of this space rather like the section "milieu" or environment in *Le Poème de l'angle droit*, it sets the scene for what is to come, it forces the reader to engage, to focus and to participate. This would be achieved through the homogenous use of materials in walls, ceiling and floor; through the absence of details that give a sense of scale; by creating geometric echoes of the vestibule itself beyond or around its boundaries and through the use of mirror and glass. William Curtis writes of the hallway of the Carpenter Centre that its "exterior features are experienced as interior ones" and that it "requires slight effort to concentrate on the room itself".[16] Sometimes it occupies a strange position within the exterior wall of the building, causing a blurring between interior and exterior space, adding to its limbo like a sense of mystery.

The vestibule often takes the form of a cube. For Le Corbusier the "closed concentric form of a circle or a square… acts profoundly on us".[17] Squares, like the platonic solids celebrated in *Vers une Architecture* (Fig. 2.14) are used constantly to give a sense of cohesiveness to a particular space. Within his office at Rue de Sèvres, Le Corbusier built a tiny little cube space to the Modulor proportion that he called "the revealing implement", 2.66 by 2.66 metres.[18] This little cube is reiterated at the entrances of several of Le Corbusier's later buildings, most notably the Maison du Brésil.

13   M. Krustrup, *Porte Email* (Copenhagen: Arkitektens Forlag, 1991).

14   Vikramaditya Prakash, *Chandigarh's Le Corbusier: The Struggle for Modernity in Postcolonial India* (Ahmedabad: Mapin, 2002), p.74.

15   See for a more extensive discussion of the symbolism of the doors at Ronchamp Flora Samuel, *Le Corbusier Architect and Feminist* (London: Wiley, 2004), pp.126–128.

16   E. Sekler and W. Curtis, *Le Corbusier at Work: The Genesis of the Carpenter Centre for the Visual Arts* (Cambridge MA: MIT, 1978), p.26.

17   Ibid., p.75.

18   *Application revelatrice*. Le Corbusier, *Œuvre Complète Volume 5, 1946–1952* (Zurich: Les Editions d'Architecture, 1973), p.185. Originally published in 1953.

4.7 **Interior of south door Notre-Dame du Haut, Ronchamp (1955).**

4.6 **Main south door of Notre-Dame du Haut, Ronchamp (1955).**

Water too is often celebrated in or near the vestibule space.[19] The act of cleansing is a universal symbol of new beginnings. At the abbey of La Thoronet, much admired by Le Corbusier, a little pavilion appended to the cloister, the lavabo, is dedicated to this act. It is my suggestion that washing held for Le Corbusier connotations of rebirth and initiation, themes central to Rabelais' description of Panurge's visit to the Oracle of the Holy Bottle in the pages of *Gargantua and Pantagruel* mentioned in the last chapter.[20]

Questioning – *savoir habiter*

The next stage in Le Corbusier's dramatic arc is less easy to describe. It occurs at the first inhabited floor level, which, certainly in the case of the piloti buildings, is a highly free-form space. In terms of Le Corbusier's rhetoric this is the point at which various options are examined and questions are asked. In his domestic architecture it forms the main living spaces, each offering a different possibility for dwelling. Sometimes playful, it offers "up the anticipation or surprise of doors which reveal unexpected space".[21] It contains within it numerous sub-routes and sub-destinations, places for rituals such as eating or contemplating the fire, and places for making decisions.

In the discussion of La Sainte Baume in the last chapter I alluded to Le Corbusier's preoccupation with the idea that the body gives access to the spiritual realm. If this is the case this questioning stage of Le Corbusier's narrative is very much about engagement with the body, the pleasures of flesh, food and conviviality, very often acting as a distraction from the main promenade. Though, as if by Ariadne's golden thread, the reader is always drawn back to the point of reorientation and the culmination of the spiritual journey.

Reorientation

Le Corbusier identifies a tendency for human beings to be "attracted towards the centre of gravity"[22] of a site which, in his buildings, nearly always takes the form of the stair or ramp, often highly contained, combined with the distant prospect of light so beautifully portrayed in the description of the Casa del Noce in Pompeii. If the questioning phase of the Le Corbusier's narrative path is about the body, this phase is about the spirit, the route to the sky.

The reader may have seen the stair at the start of the promenade, or have already travelled up one circuit of ramp, but the enticement of distant horizontal light and view upon entry to the main living level draws the reader to explore the horizontal extent of the building before being pulled back onto the promenade. There is a sense, given the initiatory impetus of Le Corbusier's architecture and his statements on the spiritual nature of domestic space,[23] that the reader is not ready for the vertical ascent until they have internalised

19   The Maison Lipchitz, the Maison Guiette in Anvers (1926) the Villa at Carthage (1929) where the sink is directly opposite the door, the Projets Wanner in Geneva (1928/29), the Immeuble pour artistes (1928/29), the apartments of Maison Locative at Alger (1933).

20   Flora Samuel, "Le Corbusier, Rabelais and the Oracle of the Holy Bottle", *Word and Image: a Journal of verbal/visual enquiry*, 16, (2000), pp.1–13.

21   Le Corbusier, *Talks with Students* (New York: Princeton Architectural Press, 2003), p.46. Originally published as *Entretien avec les étudiants des écoles d'architecture* (Paris: Denoel, 1943).

22   Le Corbusier, *Towards a New Architecture*, p.177.

23   Le Corbusier, *The Final Testament of Père Corbu*, p.91. Originally published as *Mise au Point* (Paris: Editions Forces-Vives, 1966).

4.8 **Spiral stair in the Beistegui apartment (1930) from the**
Œuvre Complète.

the meaning of the previous stage. I am reminded here of that point in Le Corbusier's rhetoric when he piles on example after example of his own work, in answer to questions from the audience, swatting away dissenters, building up momentum, tension and excitement.

Just as he evolved a limited variety of door types, Le Corbusier devised a limited variety of stair and ramp types to be reused and refined across his career.[24] These include the spiral, the dog leg, the cantilevered stair, each of which would play an integral role in the spiritual promenade. The handrails similarly come from a limited family of types. The same type of staircase is never allowed all the way up an entire building (except when the stair is secondary to the promenade) and frequently it changes position within the plan. In larger schemes such as the Unité, a whole panoply of stair types give access to the upper recesses of the roof garden – one, almost a ladder, feather light – another of solid concrete.[25]

In general, Corbusian stairs act as marker and point of reorientation, occupying a discrete role in his buildings. In the early villas, as Tim Benton observes, the spiral stair formed the "service artery passing right up through the house". This motif would "recur with a similar meaning, carrying the biomorphic analogy, whether arterial or arboreal, to quite specific conclusions".[26] In *Precisions* Le Corbusier wrote of the way in which the spiral stair, "pure vertical organ", was "inserted freely into the horizontal composition".[27] Indeed he described the stair up to the roof of the Beistegui apartment as "a screw-like staircase which does not touch the floor. If it touches it, it will break it" (Fig. 4.7).[28] Here the spiral provides a radically contrasting

24   Tim Benton, "Pessac and Lège revisited: standards, dimensions and failures", *Massilia*, 3 (2004), pp.64–99.
25   Le Corbusier, *Œuvre Complète Volume 5*, p.214.
26   Tim Benton, *The Villas of Le Corbusier 1920–1930* (London: Yale, 1987), p.143.
27   Le Corbusier, *Precisions*, pp.135 and 138.
28   Le Corbusier and Pierre Jeanneret, *Œuvre Complète Volume 2, 1929–34* (Zurich: Les Editions d'Architecture, 1995), p.57. Originally published in 1935.

4.9 **Heidi Weber Haus stair (1966).**

4.10 **A precarious stair. Villa Stein de Monzie at Garches. Still from *L'Architecture d'aujourd'hui*, Pierre Chenal (1930).**

experience of space from that of the horizontal. The spiral, as was seen in chapter 2, repeating the same archetypal course yet progressing with each cycle, was central to his conception of evolution and time. By asking the reader to mount the spiral stair, Le Corbusier is placing him or her within one of his signs, just as he planned to do at La Sainte Baume, to extraordinary effect.

A further stair, a variation of the dog leg, is one in which the treads cantilever out from either side of a concrete slab.[29] This type of stair, the discrete stand-alone tower, also finds clear expression in several other schemes, for example the early Maison Planeix, the fire stair for the Unité, and the Heidi Weber Haus (Fig. 4.9). At the Heidi Weber Haus the feeling of drama is further accentuated by the use of natural light which flows down the sides of the stair column emphasising its independence from the building as a whole. Looking upwards the light is so intense that the stair appears to continue up into the sky. This is a classic reorientation stairway. The first tread of each flight is separated conspicuously from the main structure. Its tenuous connection to reality sends messages of alarm to the visitor. The railings are very minimal, formed out of steel ribbons, they do little to engender feelings of security.

In my book *Le Corbusier in Detail* I drew attention to a sub-category of stairway, what I called "the precarious stair" (Fig. 4.10). Such stairways, frequently occurring at the summit of the promenade were, in my view designed to induce fear in those with little disposition for heights, something that Le Corbusier must have

---

29   J. Stirling, "Garches to Jaoul": Le Corbusier as Domestic Architect in 1927 and 1953" in Allen Brookes, *Archive XX*, p.x.

4.11 **Ozenfant studio (1924) from the *Œuvre Complète*.**

experienced first-hand on walks with his father in the mountains as a young boy – a fear of heights, a con-sciousness of the solidity of potential footholds, handholds, and their leverage, as well as the humbling experience of nature.

It was Eisenstein's belief that "the only means by which it is possible to make the final ideological conclusion perceptible"[30] was to take advantage of "every element that can be verified and mathematically calculated to produce certain emotional shocks in a proper order within the totality".[31] This ultimately was the "way to knowledge". Something very similar is at play in Le Corbusier's work. Ozenfant's studio, what Tim Benton calls Le Corbusier's "first exercise in the contrived and deliberately tortuous promenade architecturale", provides a case in point (Fig. 4.11).[32] Here the reader climbs a series of complex stairs, arriving at the studio only to be confronted by a ladder with double height treads allowing access to a tiny introverted and womb-like study, the experience of which would be heightened by a moment of suspense in space just prior to entry.

The precarious stair is steep. It is made of thin concrete or steel and has the appearance of folded paper. It is usually supported on a diagonal beam hidden in the shadows or cantilevered off a wall. Its railings are minimal. Ronchamp has three, for example that on the North façade.[33] The stair up to the pulpit is particu-larly unnerving, especially if negotiated under the eyes of an entire congregation (Fig. 4.1). Here the space between the ground and the first tread seems to symbolise a separation between earthly and spiritual realms (Fig. 4.12). A further precarious stair occurs on the roof of the Unité in Marseilles where the junction be-tween stair and ground is mediated by a step of the roughest concrete, giving on to treads that are almost

30   Sergei Eisenstein, "Montage of Attractions" in *The Film Sense* (London: Faber and Faber, 1943), p.181.
31   Ibid.
32   Tim Benton, *The Villas*, p.37.
33   FLC 7204, Allen Brookes, *Archive XX*, p.41.

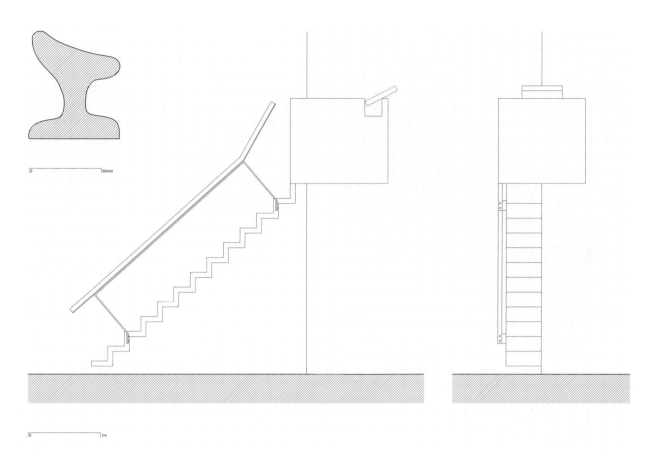

0   50mm

0   1m

4.12 **Drawing of the stair up to the pulpit of Notre-Dame du Haut, Ronchamp (1955).**

4.13 **Stair up to highest level of the Unité d'Habitation Marseilles (1952).**

shockingly hand-wrought (Figs. 4.13 and 4.14). The precarious stair plays an important role in the sequence of reorientation as it is so frightening that it forces the reader to refocus on the body and its immediate needs.

Whilst Le Corbusier was fully competent to design parapets capable of assuaging the severest case of vertigo, at times he revelled in the dramatic possibilities represented by the experience of great heights.[34] Benton writes of the Ozenfant studio:

In countless later projects, Le Corbusier built in a final stage of the progress around the house which reaches the level of danger – the steep spiral stairs on the roof of the Villa Stein or the first project for the Villa Savoye, the exposed and parapet-less roofs of the La Roche gallery wing – all these seem prepared as tests for the intrepid client and his visitors.[35]

Stairs could be rendered daunting through the solidity or flimsiness of their materials; through the presence, absence, solidity and height of handrails and risers, and of course through their position in space.

Le Corbusier thought in terms of routes which would provide an initiation into the Orphic powers of number, like that experienced by Panurge in Rabelais' *Gargantua and Pantagruel*, so it would seem to be particularly important that the stairs and ramps should be carefully proportioned to the Modulor. This is largely the case,

34   Le Corbusier was fully aware of what it was to experience vertigo. Le Corbusier, *When the Cathedrals were White* (New York: Reynal and Hitchcock, 1947), p.65. Originally published as *Quand les cathédrales étaient blanches* (Paris: Plon, 1937).

35   Tim Benton, *The Villas*, p.37.

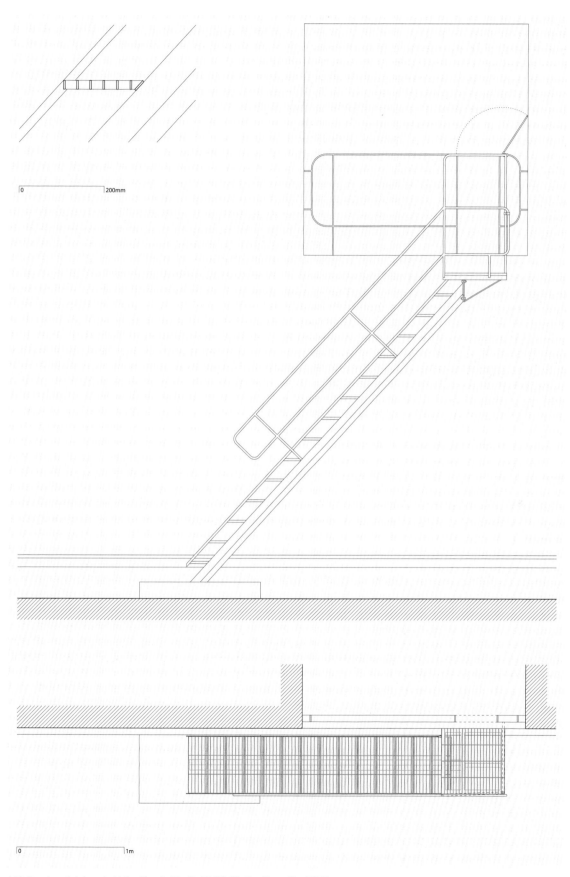

0   200mm

0   1m

4.14 **Drawing of stair up to highest level of the Unité d'Habitation Marseilles (1952).**

for example, at the Carpenter Centre (Fig. 4.15) where, in the words of Curtis, "To experience the 'promenade architecturale,' with the ramp grooves, intervals, and ratios of pilotis and other elements slipping by was also directly to perceive the kinaesthetic spatial rhythms of an architectural music – the bars and notes of Le Corbusier's 'architecture acoustique'."[36]

It is within the space of reorientation that Le Corbusier marshals his full panoply of persuasive techniques. A build-up of light inspires curiosity. Contrasts in materials stimulate the sense of touch. Unnerving gaps and spatial trickery heighten tension. The surrounding curved and bodily forms inspire sensual appreciation, while jagged treads and rough metal inspire a fear of abrasion and downfall. At the same time the use of Modulor proportions encourages a radiant dialogue between body and space.

Culmination

The promenade culminates on the roof, the completion of the spiritual axis through the building where, under ideal weather conditions, the reader is greeted with an ecstatic view of the sun or moon as the case may be. The simple attainment of rooftop space is not enough, here further choreography, particularly framing, comes into play to maximise the intensity of the experience.

A clear illustration of this moment is provided by the solarium of the Beistegui apartment the complex promenade of which culminated in a frame of four stone-clad walls open to the ceiling of the sky (Fig. 4.16). The door of the solarium was also clad in stone, meaning that when closed an immaculate flush finish would be achieved – here "the stone door recloses itself into the solarium"(Fig. 4.17).[37] Nothing would provide a distraction from the grass, the four walls and the play of clouds, the "summit" of the house an "aedicule" which is "perhaps a moving plastic event".[38] Such sculptural spaces, framing a view of the sky, would become a characteristic of Le Corbusier's architecture.

Conclusion

These are the typical constituent elements of each stage in the architectural promenade, but they are not used in the same way in every building. The following three chapters follow the development of the promenade from its confused beginnings in the Maison La Roche to its most rigid manifestation in the Villa Savoye and beyond. The early domestic schemes appear to be founded on an idea of space that is based on a series of planes while in later schemes, such as 24 Rue Nungesser et Coli and Maison Jaoul B, space is conceived of as a series of overlapping volumes working within the discipline of a vaulted structure. Here the rigidity of the Villa Savoye's narrative structure begins to be eroded, in favour of something more rich and subtle. This process receives extreme expression in the later more complex schemes, most notably the monastery of La Tourette.

---

36   E. Sekler and W. Curtis, *Le Corbusier at Work*, p.182.
37   Le Corbusier and Pierre Jeanneret, *Œuvre Complète Volume 2*, p.54.
38   Ibid.

4.15 **Ramp at Carpenter Centre (1961) from the *Œuvre Complète*.**

4.16 **Solarium of the Beistegui apartment (1930) from the *Œuvre Complète*.**

4.17 **Door into the solarium of the Beistegui apartment (1930) from the *Œuvre Complète*.**

101

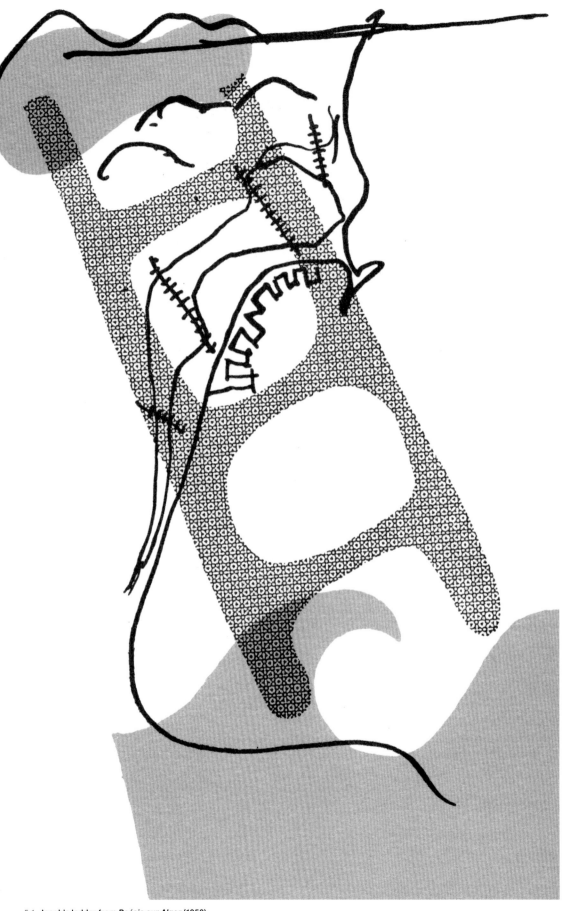

5.1 **Jacob's ladder** from *Poésie sur Alger* (1950).

5. The Jacob's Ladder Type Promenade

The Jacob's ladder route from darkness to light, provides the focus of this chapter (Fig. 5.1).[1] It is the basic promenade type. The connection between this Biblical ladder[2] and the promenade is made clear in the Maison Guiette in Anvers (1926) the stair of which is likened by Le Corbusier to "the ladder of Jacob which Charlie Chaplin climbs in The Kid" (1921).[3] Indeed it seems to me that all Le Corbusier's promenades are plays upon this original topos, a single processional route from earth to sky (Fig. 5.2) repeated.

The first explicit but slightly embryonic use of the promenade is at the Maison La Roche warranting its presence here, its tight inner city site very different to that of the wide open spaces and domino frame of the Villa Savoye, the classic Jacob's ladder promenade type, the datum for all the others. The five stages of Le Corbusier's narrative path outlined in the previous chapter are here used to foreground the particular characteristics of these two very significant journeys.

The horizontal and vertical dimensions are celebrated in the right angle at the heart of *Le Poème de l'angle droit* (Fig. 2.22) which itself takes the form of a ladder. The horizontal "complementary and natural"[4] is associated with the earth, the body, sleep and death, whilst the vertical represents action, alertness and the spiritual domain. Although Le Corbusier suggests that the trick is to establish a balance between the two, it is the vertical line as drawn in the section "tool" at the bottom of the iconostasis of the *Le Poème de l'angle droit* that ultimately takes priority, just as the sun does over water in the complex iconography of his work.[5]

MAISON LA ROCHE 1923–24

Access to the Maison La Roche is via a short walk amongst well-heeled apartment blocks from the Paris metro station at Jasmin.[6] Sited at the end of a Parisian cul de sac, the Maison La Roche is the unidentical twin of the Maison Jeanneret with which it was conceived.[7] Built for a "single man, owner of a collection of

1   See Le Corbusier *Poésie sur Alger* (Paris: Editions Connivances, 1989), p.8. Originally published in 1950.
2   Genesis, 28:11–19.
3   Le Corbusier and Pierre Jeanneret, *Œuvre Complète Volume 1, 1910–1929* (Zurich: Girsberger, 1943), p.136. Originally published in 1937. There are various edited versions of this film but the 1971 Chaplin edited version does not contain an image of the Jacob's ladder. There is however an extraordinary dream sequence in which Chaplin's alter ego the tramp dreams of his slum home translated to heaven, bedecked in flowers in which all the people that he knows have sprouted wings, including the dog. The dialectical nature of these two worlds is then broken down. It is no wonder that Le Corbusier admired Chaplin so much – including him within the images in *Le Poème Electronique* – he played with so many of the issues that Le Corbusier held dear.
4   Pierre Joffroy, "Pourquoi le plus grand architecte fut-il le plus mal aimé?", *Paris Match*, September 11, 1965. Cited in N.F. Weber, *Le Corbusier: A Life* (New York: Knopf, 2008), p.20.
5   Oddly enough the cross that Le Corbusier draws here is an inversion of the Christian crucifix as we know it.
6   Wendy Redfield has commented on the troubling absence of contextual information in historical accounts of the Maisons La Roche and Jeanneret and the Ozenfant Studio. W. Redfield, "The Supressed Site: Revealing the influence of site on two Purist works" in C.J. Burns and A. Kahn, *Site Matters: Design Concepts, Histories and Strategies* (London: Routledge, 2005), p.185–222.
7   For a comprehensive discussion of the evolution of these houses see Tim Benton, *The Villas of Le Corbusier 1920–1930* (London: Yale, 1987), pp.44–76.

5.3 **View down Rue du Docteur Blanche towards the Maison La Roche (1923–24) in 2009.**

5.4 **Tree framing the entrance of the Maison La Roche (1923–24). Photo from the *Œuvre Complète*.**

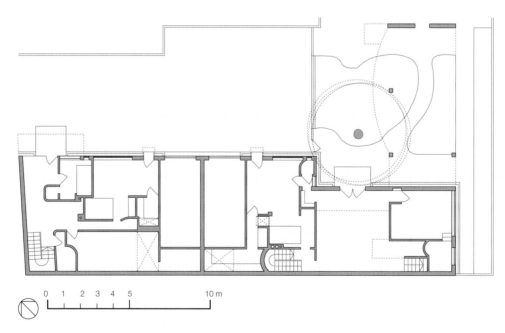

0 1 2 3 4 5   10 m

5.5 **Plan of the ground floor of the Maison La Roche (1923–24).**

5.2 **The climax of the promenade at the Villa Stein de Monzie at Garches. Still from *L'Architecture d'aujourd'hui*, Pierre Chenal (1930).**

modern art and passionate about artistic things" it was in Le Corbusier's terms "a little like a promenade architecturale".[8] Although Le Corbusier here uses rather tentative language, perhaps reflecting the fact that the concept of the promenade was not yet fully formulated in his mind, his description of the route through the building is extremely precise.

One enters: the architectural spectacle then offers itself to the gaze; one follows an itinerary and the perspectives develop with great variety; one plays with the influx of light brightening the walls or creating shadows. The bays open perspectives onto the exterior where one finds the architectural unity. On the interior the first essays in polychromie, based on specific reactions to colours allow the "architectural camouflage", that is to say the affirmation of certain volumes or in contrast, their effacement. The interior of the house must be white, but in order for that to be appreciable, a well-regulated polychromy is needed; the walls in shadow will be blue, those in bright light will be red.[9]

It is clear from this statement that Le Corbusier thought of the building as an essay in space, using perspective, volumes, light and colour to create a varied sequence of experiences that draw attention to the possibilities of a world beyond the immediately visible, ineffable space.

Threshold

The walk down the quiet lane of Rue du Docteur Blanche calms the mind and heightens expectations of what is to come, the almost Palladian façade viewed at the end of the vista of the street, obscured only by the trunk of a very large tree (Fig. 5.3) which is of great importance to the overall schema. Having passed through the simple steel gateway into the forecourt the reader is inflected to the door by the curve of the gallery while the tree, to the left of the gate, forms one corner of an implied space prefacing the entrance to the house (Fig. 5.4). This is not the most elegant or clear of Le Corbusier's entrance sequences as the pilotis look as though they should shelter the main entrance door. Instead priority has been given to placing the entry to the building at the triple height hinge that separates the gallery and library side of the building from that devoted to dwelling. (Fig. 5.5)

The simple double doors of the Maison La Roche are given presence by their shape, by the large, rather Roman knobs at the centre of each and by the concrete mat well that projects before them. Inside the doorway is protected by the soffit of the walkway that passes overhead, giving depth to the threshold and

8   Le Corbusier and Pierre Jeanneret *Œuvre Complète Volume 1*, p.60.
9   Ibid.

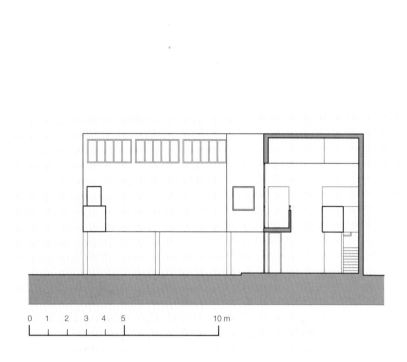

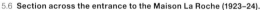

0 1 2 3 4 5   10 m

5.6 **Section across the entrance to the Maison La Roche (1923–24).**

5.7 **Blue wall to the left of the main door. Maison La Roche (1923–24).**

an unexpected presence to the doors that appear so minimal from without (Fig. 5.6). This strongly transverse space is open at either end. As a result the horizontal band feels taut, extending beyond the boundaries of the space holding and protecting the reader before entry. The walls at its outer limits are painted a deep and shocking blue, just as described in the quote above, bringing forward that which would have receded into gloom (Fig. 5.7). At the same time the floor surface of small white tiles set diagonally to the walls erodes the force of the horizontal band with its forward inflection of tiny but insistent lines.

Sensitising Vestibule

Although the extent of the vestibule is very unclear in this scheme its sensitising function is dramatically expressed by the full triple height of the entrance hall, the sheer expanse of which is felt all the more keenly by the reader emerging from beneath the walkway that runs above the entrance (Fig. 5.8). Deborah Gans writes:

Carefully placed wall openings, stairs and balconies divide the space and surfaces of the hall into layers with implied axes in a kind of three-dimensional plaid. … The promenade orchestrates movement across these layers in relation to fixed moments such as balconies.[10]

Used in Le Corbusier's time as a receptacle of art, the room itself engages in spatial games within the paintings themselves and is designed to confuse and fascinate.

The backlit stairway to the library and gallery above thrusts forward into the hallway whilst the stairway to the roof garden is tucked away behind a wall (Fig. 5.9). Their relative widths, 880 mm for the former and 780 mm for the latter, only serve to reinforce the subservience of the roof garden route, although their handrail details are the same in both cases (Fig. 5.10). The secondary route to the roof garden (Fig. 5.11) up through the living spaces of the house provides nothing like the focus of the primary route to be discussed here.

10 Deborah Gans, *The Le Corbusier Guide* (Princeton: Princeton Architectural Press, 2006), p.58.

5.11 **Roof garden over dwelling sides of the Maison La Roche (1923–24).**
Photograph taken in 2009 as refurbishment work was being completed.

5.8 **The main hallway of the Maison La Roche (1923–24).**

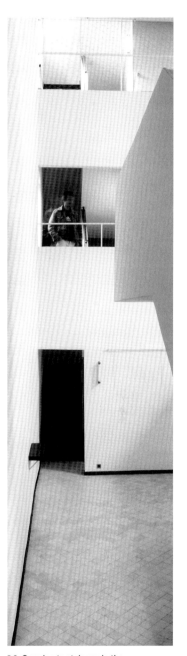

5.10 **Handrail on stair at**
Maison La Roche (1923–24).

5.9 **Opening to stairway in the**
residential side of the
Maison La Roche (1923–24).

5.12 **View towards gallery at first floor level of the Maison La Roche (1923–24).**

5.13 **Entrance to the gallery of the Maison La Roche (1923–24).**

Questioning – *savoir habiter*

On entry into the main hall movement is clearly inflected towards the left, up the gallery stair, taking the reader away from the main hall before being shot back into it at first floor level by a little projecting balcony and a further vestibule space that seems to mark the real point of entry to the building, as in the *piano nobile* of a Renaissance palace (Fig. 5.12). There are decisions to be made here – whether to cross the balcony to the dwelling side of the house, past the vast window and the view of the tree, or to slide into La Roche's gallery which, when open, is announced by a burst of light but, when closed, is hidden firmly by solid dark double doors.

Something that adds to the richness of the space is the treatment of thresholds which are rarely clear and distinct. The entrance to the gallery, for example, is complicated by changes in floor finish and the overhang of the balcony above (Fig. 5.13). In the centre is a black stone table, a precursor to some of the distinctly altar-like tables in Le Corbusier's later work. It is set into a shiny black square of flooring that reinforces its importance within the space. To the left a steep ramp curves up along the outer wall of the room (Figs. 5.14 and 5.15). Beneath it a very odd sliver of mirror creates the impression that the ramp is a continuous curve arcing down into some illusory space (Fig. 5.16).

Clearly the gallery, any gallery, should be designed with the aim of provoking thought. Hung with painted work by Le Corbusier and his contemporaries La Roche's gallery would constitute an essay into the possibilities of space. Although La Roche and Le Corbusier were to remain firm friends, the art collector entered into altercations with Le Corbusier about the hanging of his paintings, a subject upon which he had very strong feelings. Christopher Pearson writes that "in Le Corbusier's theory, the work of art was only effective in radiating its metaphysical presence when placed in an isolated position of dominance, at some remove from distracting elements".[11] So, perhaps ironically for a house designed as a gallery, Le Corbusier insisted

11   C.E.M. Pearson,"Integrations of Art and Architecture in the work of Le Corbusier. Theory and Practice from Ornamentalism to the 'Synthesis of the Major Arts'". Unpublished PhD thesis, Stanford University (1995), p.91.

5.15 Gallery of the Maison La Roche (1923–24).

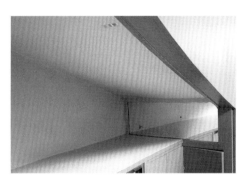

5.16 Sliver of mirror beneath the ramp of the gallery of
Maison La Roche (1923–24).

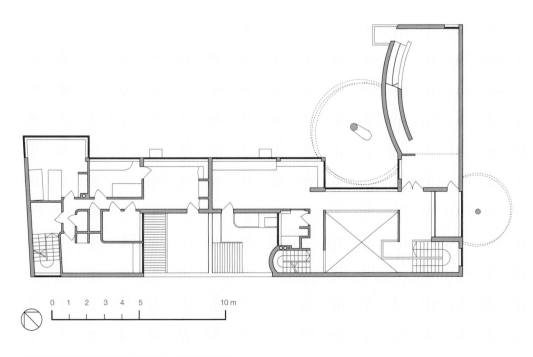

0 1 2 3 4 5   10 m

5.14 Plan of the first floor of the Maison La Roche (1923–24).

5.17 **The trees at front and back of the Maison La Roche (1923–24) act as the main points of orientation.**

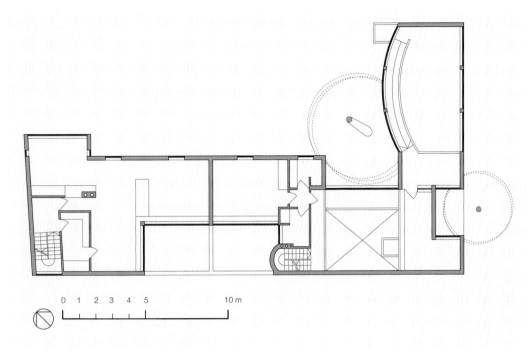

5.18 **Plan of second floor of the Maison La Roche (1923–24).**

"absolutely" that certain parts of the architecture should remain free of paintings[12] leading his highly astute client to complain: "I commissioned from you a 'frame for my collection'. You provided me with a 'poem of walls'. Which of us two is most to blame?"[13] The building was designed very largely as a unified narrative, complete in itself without the distraction of the diverse set of paintings that it was ostensibly designed to display.

Reorientation

As the stairs and ramps in this building shift unexpectedly around the plan, the main points of orientation are instead the two trees that hem the building in, one at the front and one at the back (Fig. 5.17). Enigmatically Le Corbusier writes that "it is here on the exterior that one finds the architectural unity".[14] Both trees appear prominently on all plans, the drawings even indicating the incline of their trunks (Fig. 5.18). These "ancient trees to be respected"[15] seem to be of fundamental importance to the conceptual framework of the house, the tree being one of the staples of Le Corbusier's symbolic diet. Significantly the scheme that follows on from the Maison La Roche in the *Œuvre Complète*, the Maison Lipchitz, is similarly tree-focussed. At the Maison La Roche the trees act as points of orientation in the highly complex space.

---

12   Tim Benton, *The Villas*, p.63.
13   Dossier La Roche, Doc 506 bis, 24 May 1926 quoted in ibid., p.71.
14   Le Corbusier and Pierre Jeanneret, *Œuvre Complète Volume 1*, p.60
15   Ibid., p.64.

5.19 **The rooflight in the library of the Maison La Roche (1923–24), just visible from the ground floor hallway.**

5.20 **Study of the Maison La Roche (1923–24).**

Culmination

A further point of orientation is the rooflight of the library, just visible when standing in the hallway (Fig. 5.19). In Le Corbusier's ascetic world the library, accessed via the spatial complexities of the gallery space, provides the true culmination of this journey into knowledge (Fig. 5.20). In *Le Corbusier in Detail* I set out a taxonomy of Corbusian rooflights. This particular rooflight is most emphatically designed for the viewing of the sky as well as the ingress of illumination, a pure square of blue with clouds scudding unimpeded by details of frame, latch or mullion.

Summary

The Maison La Roche provides a good illustration of the architectural promenade at an early stage in its development, before Le Corbusier was aware of its full potential. Here the stages of the dramatic arc are quite difficult to delineate as they do not yet appear with the clarity of later schemes (Fig. 5.21). Le Corbusier wrote of the "torments"[16] of the composition, the strict constraints of the site which come through very clearly in Tim Benton's account of the development of the project.[17] Clearly Le Corbusier was fully aware of some of the weaknesses I have described in the route, such as the fact that the main entry does not occur beneath the pilotis and the absence of a clear reorienting stairway. It is the fragility of the resolution in this house that makes it so very tantalising.

16 Ibid.
17 Tim Benton, *The Villas*, pp.43–75.

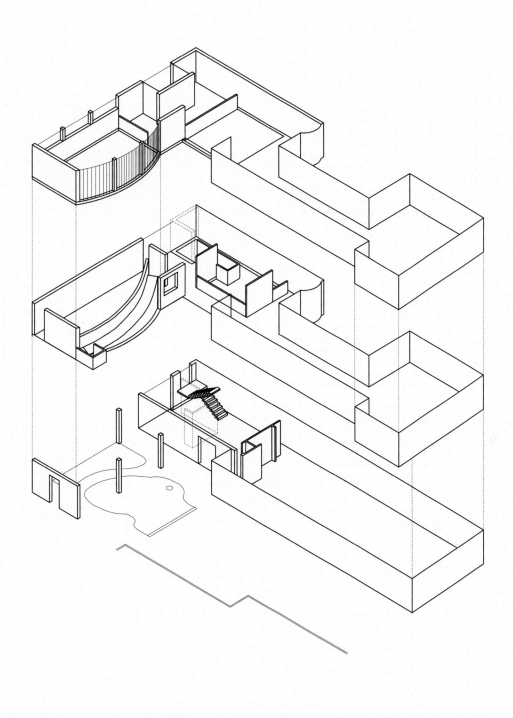

5.21 **Isometric drawing showing the elements of the architectural promenade in the Maison La Roche (1923–24).**

VILLA SAVOYE 1929–31

So well-known is this villa that it is quite difficult to look at it once again from first principles, clearing the mind of the vast amount of commentary that it brings with it, some of which is synthesised here.[18] Of particular interest is Josep Quetglas' account of Le Corbusier's plans to modify the building into a "museum Corbu" after its neglect during World War II. The proposed changes here include a large mural over the garage door, an enamelled door replete with Corbusian symbolism and a radical change in colour scheme – all of which would have brought to the fore the initiatory aspects of the building that receive only embryonic expression in its first incarnation.[19]

Threshold

Built within an expanse of grass bordering onto woodland, the Villa Savoye was envisaged ostensibly as an experiment in housing. The precise threshold of the building is the simple doorway that appears beneath the piloti, but a good deal of spatial gymnastics have already been performed to get to this point. In a tiny axonometric drawing in the *Œuvre Complète* a road can be seen entering beneath the pilotis on one side and exiting on the other (Fig. 5.22). It is well known that the building was designed for approach by car, past the tiny modernist lodge semi-obscured by a startling rough stone wall (Fig. 5.23), past a fringe of trees that mask it from view, and then out into the open in full view of the southlight glare of the façade before entering the gloom of the pilotis (Fig. 5.24). Accommodation at ground level – laundry, garages and other service spaces are painted green on the exterior to suppress their importance in the scheme of things.[20] The car then curves around to the left allowing the viewer glimpses of the entry hall through vertically striated glass – a precursor to the ondulatoire – to arrive at the enigmatic doorway at the very centre of the arc in a, seemingly perfect, synergy of house and car. "It is the minimum turning circle of a car that apparently governs the dimensions of the whole thing," writes Le Corbusier. One of the photographs in the *Œuvre Complète* is entitled "the car returns towards Paris" suggesting that this particular promenade at least really begins at the heart of that city.[21]

With great perversity the entrance to the Villa Savoye appears on the dark, northern side opposite to the main approach (Fig. 5.25). The car argument does not really suffice to explain this move, justification for which must lie in Le Corbusier's desire to stimulate curiosity and to prepare the reader for the switch back experience of space that is to follow. The door into the hall, whilst being slightly lost in the sweeping arc of the ground floor plan (Fig. 5.26), is given stature by its central position and the depth of its threshold. The thing that assists the door most in the accrual of gravitas is the fact that it is set just forward of a series of pilotis meaning that the building is entered through columns as in a Greek temple. Like the Maison La Roche the transverse push of the pilotis extending to either side competes with the impetus forward making more of an event of the door itself.

---

18   For a comprehensive study of the history of this project see Tim Benton, *The Villas*, pp.190–207.

19   Josep Quetglas, *Le Corbusier, Pierre Jeanneret: Villa Savoye 'Les Heures Claires' 1928–1963* (Madrid: Rueda, 2004).

20   Colour would allow certain parts of the building to blend into the landscape, "the foliage of the gardens and of the forest". Le Corbusier and Pierre Jeanneret *Œuvre Complète Volume 1*, p.86.

21   Le Corbusier and Pierre Jeanneret, *Œuvre Complète Volume 2, 1929–34* (Zurich: Les Editions d'Architecture, 1995), p.26. Originally published in 1935.

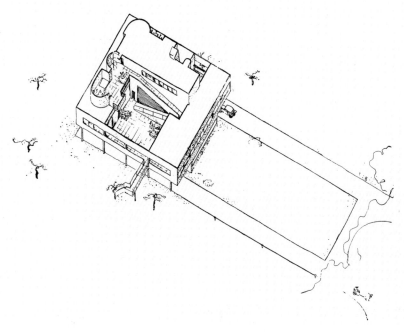

5.22 **Axonometric drawing from the *Œuvre Complète* showing the route of the car beneath the pilotis.**

5.24 **View of Villa Savoye (1929–31) from approach.**

5.23 **Gate house of the Villa Savoye (1929–31).**

115

5.25 **Villa Savoye (1929–31) entrance façade.**

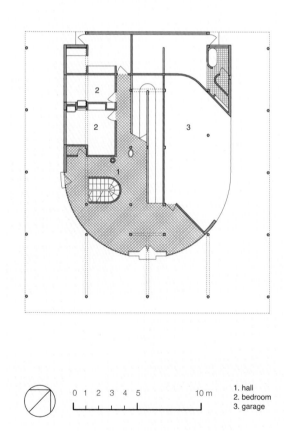

0 1 2 3 4 5   10 m

1. hall
2. bedroom
3. garage

5.26 **Plan of the ground floor of the Villa Savoye (1929–31).**

5.27 **Villa Savoye (1929–31) entrance façade.**

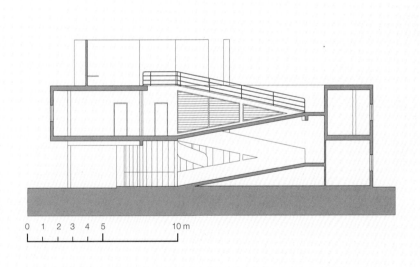

5.28 **Section across the Villa Savoye (1929–31).**

Something that is conspicuously left out of the plans of the Villa Savoye and out of many accounts of this building are the dotted lines of the overhanging beams and other aerial events that contribute to the experience of the whole (Fig. 5.27). At the entrance to the house a system of pilotis and beams runs roughly north-south in the direction of the main route contributing to the directional thrust within the building. What is most odd is that the door itself appears to be positioned on one of the main structural lines of the house meaning that a beam passes directly over its centre point (Fig. 5.28). Further, although the exterior gives the illusion that the structural grid is even and uniform throughout the building, the size of the bay decreases at the entrance. The result is a close clustering of columns at the entrance something that adds to the authority of the door whilst playing tricks with the reader's sense of spatial order.

5.29 **The "entry vestibule" of the Villa Savoye (1929) from the** *Œuvre Complète*.

5.30 **The basin in the entry vestibule of the Villa Savoye (1929) from the** *Œuvre Complète*.

Sensitising Vestibule

The hall is a confusing space of highly indeterminate shape (Fig. 5.29). It feels like it is bleeding away at its edges, an impression that is assisted by the use of Le Corbusier's favourite white 20cm tiles set on the diagonal. Beyond the matwell the inner edge of the ramp lines up with the central line of the door. To the left a spiral stair is orientated away from the entrance to discourage immediate usage. The authority of the ramp is frail, achieved largely through its central position and its proximity to the tiny basin which gives the space a human scale and a presence that it would otherwise lack (Fig. 5.30). It is uncommonly like a holy water stoop on entrance into a church, causing Colin Rowe to comment:

As we further enter the vestibule of this temple and house, just how are we intended to interpret the so prominently displayed lavabo or sink? Scarcely as a functional accessory. For any details which one might associate with the act of washing (towels and soap) are conspicuously absent and would surely damage the pristine impact of this very obsessive little statement. Is it then a place of ritual purification, the equivalent of a holy water stoop? Personally, I think that it is…[22]

The configuration of elements has here been delicately judged. If the sink were a few centimetres to the right all the impetus of the promenade would plough down the corridor and into the laundry, indeed the lines of the tiles encourage the reader to do so.

Differentiation between major and minor rooms is not achieved through detail, but through the positioning of doors. Here the doors of the servants' rooms are kept away from the main body of the hall space. The colour of the walls assists in suppressing the importance of the service corridor which is a dull brown that does little to excite the heart or encourage the ingress of light. So perverse is Le Corbusier in his thinking that it is tempting to imagine that the minor spaces and routes, the ones that have been repressed and screened off, are perhaps the truly important spaces, the earthy Sancho Panza servant spaces to the more idealistic Don Quixote promenade. Certainly it is important to emphasise that one could not exist without the other.

22   Colin Rowe, *The Architecture of Good Intentions* (London: Academy Editions, 1994), p.60.

5.31 **View down ramp to door of Villa Savoye (1929–31).**

5.32 **The visual connection between the first floor and the ground floor of the Villa Savoye (1929–31) across the ramp.**

On the ramp the space expands upwards pulling the reader along with it (Fig. 5.31). Le Corbusier describes it as "very gentle", moving "imperceptibly up a storey".[23] For José Baltanás it "transforms walking into ritual, dignifying the space, while also metynomically evoking the machine age by introducing the ramp-road into a domestic interior".[24] Everything is done to ease the transition to the upper floor. The space of the ground floor and the hanging garden above are conflated in section, the two floors connected by shafts of light that beam down from above and are reflected in the corridor wall below. (Fig. 5.32)

Questioning – *savoir habiter*

At the top of the ramp there is no direct view into the living room, making it feel slightly peripheral to the overall scheme of the promenade (Fig. 5.33). The door into this space is however glazed, unlike any of the other doors in the building, so it does offer the reader an oblique glimpse into the possibilities of the living spaces of the first floor. Entering through it, the eyes are pulled to the left along the panorama of the horizontal windows on the outer wall into a spiralling trajectory that leads you back to the fully glazed wall of the hanging garden with a view of the ramp leading up to the roof. There is no direct means of access to this space so it is necessary instead to return to the landing.

From here the walls of ancillary spaces, such as bedrooms, that face onto the hall are painted dark colours, brown and dark blue causing them to recede into the background. The door to the master bedroom is, for example, set into a brown wall, guarded from the main landing by a piloti and the convex curve of the spiral stair (Fig. 5.34). The subroutes into the bedrooms parallel the movement of the ramp and are lit strategically with roof lights in a manner that has little impact upon the main promenade. An intriguing detail occurs at the end of the route to one of the bedrooms. Here, when the doors into the bathroom and the door into the bedroom are opened up, a single door jamb, like a fulcrum post at the end of a Roman racetrack, makes a very odd space of reflected doors, encouraging the reader to swerve round and back towards whence he or she came. (Fig. 5.35)

23   Le Corbusier and Pierre Jeanneret, *Œuvre Complète Volume 1*, p.187.
24   José Baltanás, *Walking through Le Corbusier: A Tour of his Masterworks* (London: Thames and Hudson, 2005), p.6.

5.33 **Door to the hanging garden of the Villa Savoye (1929–31) from the Œuvre Complète.**

5.34 **View across landing of the Villa Savoye (1929–31) towards the master bedroom showing how particular routes are repressed.**

When in the ancillary spaces of the Villa Savoye, when trying to understand the meaning of this building, the reader is constantly subject to a mild but insistent call back on to the landing. This is caused by the use of colour – similar colours being used for example on a bedroom wall and on the landing beyond causing a contraction of space between the two as the eye conflates the colours. It is caused by the constant pull of the horizontal windows on the outer wall which make the eye slide sideways and then round corners pulling our vision back to where we came from. It is caused by the transverse progress of pilotis and beams which, even when they occur in an enclosed bedroom, are part of a system that marches back into the landing, the centre of gravity of the building.

The door to the hanging garden is immediately to the left of the reader as he or she arrives at the top of the ramp so it feels more accessible than the living room door (Fig. 5.36). Unlike the living room door this one is solid, set within a broad masonry frame that gives it greater presence than it would have had if it had been simply set into glass. At the same time the glazing all around the frame allows spatial flow between the landing and the hanging garden itself. This is a door configuration that Le Corbusier would return to repeatedly.

The square plan form of the hanging garden, as in many Le Corbusier buildings, gives it an innate authority (Fig. 5.37). The floor of the roof garden is slightly higher than that of the hall, meaning that there is a step up between them. The tiles at landing level are still on the diagonal encouraging movement across the space, but once inside the roof garden the floor slabs are orthogonal, giving a real sense of arrival and order. Yet Le Corbusier chips away at the space with a full battery of techniques to cause visual confusion.

The hanging garden of the Villa Savoye is a very strange space full of details that deceive the eye. Primary amongst these must be the altar-like table that sits at right angles to the horizontal frame in the outer wall (Fig. 5.38). I have always read this as a dining table ready to be set with wine, bread and all the accoutrements of a pleasant meal, but it would be absolutely impossible to use the table in this way as it is far too low for any adult to sit at. In height it is more suitable for a seat than a table, but then again it is slightly too high for

5.35 **When all the doors are opened the route swerves around the doorframe of this bedroom in the Villa Savoye (1929–31).**

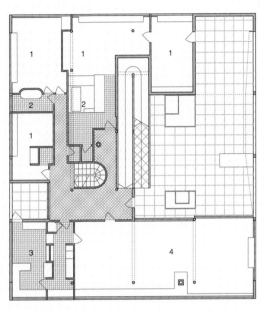

0 1 2 3 4 5   10 m

1. bedroom
2. bathroom
3. kitchen
4. living

5.36 **Plan of the first floor of the Villa Savoye (1929–31).**

5.38 **Table in hanging garden of Villa Savoye (1929–31).**

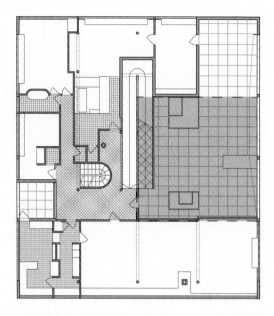

5.37 **Diagram showing implied square of hanging garden.**

that. If we assume that it is at a reasonable height for a table then our whole sense of the scale of the hanging garden changes and we are deceived into thinking it much larger than it actually is. A further oddity is the beam that stiffens the top part of the empty horizontal opening in the wall. This chamfers out at the centre before thinning back into the corners – almost like an inverted bay window, giving the top cord of the window opening a stiffness both real and visual. Another trick is the sneaky extension of the glazing beyond the pilotis on the corner of the living room, the strangeness of which defies photography. These things and others incite questions upon the nature and meaning of space in this curious building.

Reorientation

The ramp of the Villa Savoye provides a reorientation point par excellence. Mention here must be made of the handrail, whose smooth curves invite the hand, set inconspicuously within the white plastered plane of the balustrade (Fig. 5.39). Its sense of solidity and scale means that it acts as a serious point of reorientation in this shifting world. On the first ramp up to the solarium its opacity gives enclosure to the hanging garden below. This contrasts with the balustrade of the upper flight of the ramp which is formed out of slim railings. Once again the tile of the ramp is set on the diagonal to provide onward impetus. The height of the wall surrounding the landing at half level has been carefully construed to prevent outward views and to encourage continued progress up to the solarium roof garden with the warm sun on one's back. As with the sink in the ground floor entrance hall, the ramp is given visual anchorage by the presence of a large pure white chimney stack at roof level, which appears like nothing so much as a lone column amongst the shards of an ancient Greek ruin.

Culmination

The importance of the stack in the composition of the route is manifest in the photograph entitled "promenade architecturale" in the *Œuvre Complète* (Fig. 5.40). The climax here, very clearly, is the empty frame, deceptively low in the wall that appears immediately beyond the swoop of the ramp (Fig. 5.41). A curved wall, it acts like a buffer against the momentum of the promenade – the concave surface providing maximum resistance in Le Corbusier's taxonomy of aerodynamics. Yet punctured into that surface is a hole, an empty frame –

5.39 Handrail of ramp up to the roof garden of the Villa Savoye (1929–31).

5.40 "Promenade architecturale": the ramp up to the solarium of the Villa Savoye (1929–31) from the *Œuvre Complète*.

5.41 Final frame of the promenade in the roof garden solarium of the Villa Savoye (1929–31).

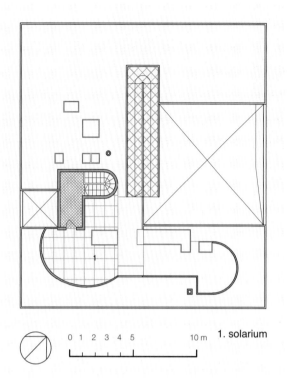

0 1 2 3 4 5   10 m **1. solarium**

5.42 **Plan of the roof terrace of the Villa Savoye (1929–31).**

given a certain extra depth by the small strip of roof that extends beyond it – through which all the pent-up energy of the promenade is spilled (Fig. 5.42).

Le Corbusier gives a strong clue about the promenade of the Villa Savoye in the *Œuvre Complète* where, as "the orientation of the sun is opposed to that of the view", it is necessary "to go and find the sun" in the solarium which "crowning the ensemble", is "a very rich architectural element".[25] This then is the focus of the promenade. It is at this point that the opposing tension between the view, through the final frame of the promenade, and the direction of the sun is felt most keenly. Finding the sun, central message of Le Corbusier's inner world, is thus central to the narrative of the promenade.

There is also an issue here to do with the anticipation and echo of events, prolepsis, that can be seen in some of the most complex promenade sequences.[26] Shapes, lighting conditions, compositions that appear at one stage in the promenade are then repeated later on in a slightly different format, recalling past events and suggesting others yet to come. An example is the ramp of the Villa Savoye which is closely contained at either end by solid walls. The opening up of the solarium at the end of the route feels all the more special when set against a backdrop of memories of enclosure below. Further, the use of a limited family of forms gives unity to the space and a unity to the experience therein.

25 Le Corbusier and Pierre Jeanneret, *Œuvre Complète Volume 1*, p.187.
26 Colin Rowe and Robert Slutsky, "Transparency: Literal and Phenomenal" in Colin Rowe, *The Mathematics of the Ideal Villa* (Cambridge MA: MIT, 1976), pp.159–183.

5.43 **Woman walking up to the solarium of the Villa Savoye. Still from *L'Architecture d'aujourd'hui*, Pierre Chenal (1930).**

Summary

There is no clearer example of the classic Jacob's ladder route than the Villa Savoye which represents a maturing of Le Corbusier's thinking upon the subject of the promenade. The elements of the route are legible and visible from one stage to another, the ramp up the building providing the backbone of the experience that is on offer.

The narrative of Pierre Chenal's 1930 film *Architecture d'aujourd'hui*, originally with subtitles by Le Corbusier and a sound track by Pierre Jeanneret, provides evidence of a similar narrative to the one described above. It begins with a locating shot of the Villa Savoye from the ground level garden moving up and along the ribbon windows that open onto the living room and the first floor hanging garden beyond. Referring to the way the eye can pan across the view, Kenneth Frampton writes of the "cinematic effect" of this window type from the inside.[27] Here it is used in reverse.

The shot provides a clue as to where the camera will be positioned next, another garden space, the hanging garden itself, where it tilts and pans along and up the ramp to the rooftop solarium, in this way following the promenade from ground to roof. The shot feels full of potential, waiting for human contact to make sense of these abstract forms and spaces. Next the camera is positioned at rooftop level looking down on a woman as she comes through the door into the hanging garden and starts walking briskly up the ramp, her face in full view (Fig. 5.43). Then, with a trick of continuity, the woman is seen walking up the same portion of ramp – this time from within the stairwell from which we have just seen her emerge, as though reliving her experience from that angle. Eisenstein's ideas on parallax – the change of position of the body, hence with its perception, due to a change of position of the observer – come into play. Here particular parts of the building can be viewed in a series of different ways at different points on the promenade. Yves-Alain Bois writes of the "decentering" effect of this experience.[28] With further editorial sleight of hand the camera then returns to the ramp to catch the woman's back as she strides up to the solarium window, the climax of the house. The emphasis of the shot is on her hand moving along the delightfully curved handrail which occupies the middle of the frame.

27   Kenneth Frampton, *Studies in Tectonic Culture: The Poetics of Construction in Nineteenth and Twentieth Century Architecture* (Cambridge MA: MIT, 1996), p.144.

28   Sergei Eisenstein, Yves-Alain Bois, Michael Glenny, "Montage and Architecture" (c.1937), *Assemblage*, 10 (1989), p.113.

The woman, now being filmed at rooftop level, is seen taking a chair and moving it into a position, hidden from us by plants, from which she can appreciate the view. She settles down to enjoy the ultimate experience that the house has to offer (Fig. 5.44). Then, in an echo of the very first locating shot, the camera is positioned back down in the garden looking at the solarium window from below. From here it is moved further back into the woods, but it still looks at the same window, a reminder of the viewpoint of the woman who sits in comfort unseen behind the frame. Despite the fact that a limited number of different shots are used by Chenal the screen geography of the space is extremely clear. The camera angles suggest a sequence of sunny spaces, each leading on from one to the other, which are stitched together by the movements of the body. It is impossible in film to show a person progressing up a house in one shot, continuity techniques are needed to make sense of the sequences and the changing position of the camera. It is the absence, then presence of the person that makes it far more poignant.

Similar formats are followed in Chenal's study of the Villa Church and the Villa at Garches also included within the film. What does this tell us about the intentions of the promenade? Firstly that the linking of major spaces with the outside world is an absolute priority and needs to be done as quickly as possible; secondly that the building is in some way incomplete without the presence of people. Further the detail of hand on rail and foot on tread gives some sense of the importance of tactile issues to the experience of the route, a dance between the woman and her surroundings.

Conclusion

The Maison La Roche marks an early stage in the evolution of the Jacob's ladder type promenade. Although there is a clear route from earth to sky, the stages of the dramatic arc are not clear and orientation around the building is confusing, unlike the Villa Savoye, in which the Jacob's ladder reads extremely clearly and the journey conforms well to Le Corbusier's narrative path.

The structure of the Maison La Roche appears to be supported partly on columns and partly on walls, whilst the Villa Savoye is largely a domino frame meaning that Le Corbusier had more freedom in the distribution of the elements of the promenade. The next chapter focuses on two vaulted schemes revealing more about the impact of structure upon the character of the route that it contains.

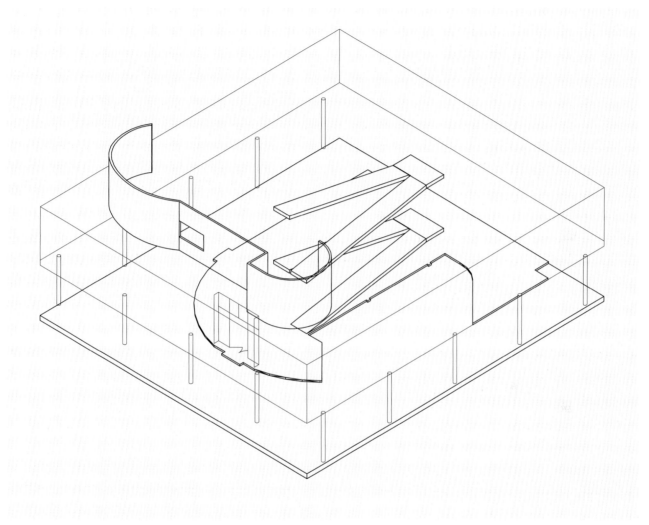

5.44 **Isometric showing the elements of the promenade in the Villa Savoye (1929–31).**

6.1 **Vault in the studio of the penthouse, 24 Rue Nungesser et Coli.**

6. Overlapping Narratives of Domestic Space

In the last chapter I described the evolution of the Jacob's ladder route in Le Corbusier's domestic work culminating in the Villa Savoye, where the journey from earth to sky can be felt most clearly. This chapter focuses on the development of this topos in two vaulted schemes, the penthouse at 24 Rue Nungesser et Coli and the Maison Jaoul B. In the former the volumes work across the grain of the vaults resulting in a more stuttering sensation of space than that in the latter where the promenade is in the same direction as the vault itself. The task here is to contain the relentless flow of movement. Mapping the routes through these buildings against the stages of Le Corbusier's dramatic arc reveals a growing complexity in his thinking about what the promenade might actually be.

PENTHOUSE, FLAT 7, 24 RUE NUNGESSER ET COLI 1933

Home to Le Corbusier and his wife Yvonne, the penthouse at 24 Rue Nungesser et Coli occupies the two top floors of his Porte Molitor Block in the Auteuil district of Paris (Fig. 6.2). The apartment dates from the same period that Le Corbusier was developing ideas for *La Ville Radieuse* and should be seen as an increment of that plan which he wrote of in terms of a balance between masculine and feminine elements.

This prodigious spectacle has been produced by the interplay of two elements, one male, one female: sun and water. Two contradictory elements that both need the other to exist...[1]

Adhering to old stereotypes[2] Le Corbusier defined "male" architecture as "strong objectivity of forms, under the intense light of a Mediterranean sun", while "female" architecture was described in terms of "limitless subjectivity rising against a clouded sky",[3] in other words, something more nebulous.[4] Le Corbusier's architecture became a marriage of these two opposites, in alchemical terms, a highly charged and erotic interplay intended to work upon the inhabitant through what he called a "psychophysiology" of the feelings.[5] At 24 Rue Nungesser et Coli he created a dwelling for the man and woman of the "machine age", mirroring and reinforcing the interplay of the masculine and feminine life within the apartment.[6]

---

1   Le Corbusier, *The Radiant City* (London, Faber, 1967), p.78. Originally published as *La Ville Radieuse* (Paris: Editions de l'Architecture d'Au-jourd'hui, 1935).

2   See "On Difference: Masculine and Feminine" in A. Forty, *Words and Buildings* (London: Thames and Hudson, 2000), pp.42–61 for a discussion of the enduring tendency to see architecture in terms of gender.

3   Le Corbusier, *Modulor* (London: Faber, 1954), p.224. Originally published as *Le Modulor* (Paris: Editions d'Architecture d'Aujourd'hui, 1950).

4   Pearson writes of the way in which Le Corbusier distributed gendered artworks within his clients' houses, for example in the Villas Stein and Mandrot. "At the Mandrot villa… the association of the female form with passivity and nature and the male form with a more active dominance of its surroundings is more typical of Le Corbusier's masculinist symbology." Pearson, "Integrations of Art and Architecture in the Work of Le Corbusier", PhD thesis, Stanford University (1995), p.139.

5   Le Corbusier, *Modulor*, p.113.

6   See Flora Samuel, "Animus, Anima and the Architecture of Le Corbusier", *Harvest*, 48, 2 (2003), pp.42–60 for a Jungian interpretation of this argument.

6.2 **24 Rue Nungesser et Coli (1933).**

6.3 **Front door at ground level of 24 Rue Nungesser et Coli (1933).**

Threshold

To reach Rue Nungesser et Coli, most appropriately named after a well-known aviator, you emerge from the metro at Auteuil, as Le Corbusier would have done on his way home from work, cross a series of large boulevards and skirt around a sports stadium before arriving in this quiet street of apartment blocks. Access to the penthouse and the other apartments in the building, is achieved via a delicious bronze handle set into an oversized metal door (Fig. 6.3). The façade of the building onto the street appears entirely orthogonal yet the mat well is skewed slightly so that, even when one is standing at the front door, subliminal messages are received about the direction of the route through the building via the feet and eyes. The lofty communal hall (Fig. 6.4) is dissected by a warped line of columns that slurp the reader between curved walls towards the mirrored lift shaft, through a door, over an odd little stream of glass block (Fig. 6.5) and into the dark and deeply ordinary Parisian light well upon which all the vertical circulation is situated.[7] From here the reader curls and recurls up the highly constrained dogleg stair to arrive at the top, a dizzy pilgrim at a door which is marked only by a stencilled number 7 (Fig. 6.6). It can be no accident, given that the flat belonged to a deeply superstitious man who always sat in the same seat number on aeroplanes, that it is numbered 7. Like *Le Poème de l'angle droit* the building has seven layers, seven signifying the union of body and spirit, in other words harmony.

---

7   Deborah Gans notes that the placement of structure at the centre of the building is a strategy adopted in the Maison Cook and elsewhere, but whereas "at Cook the circulation adapts to the column location, at Porte Molitor the demands of the promenade appear to warp the column line. The entrance is shifted in relation to the center column; but on the interior, the lobby columns appear staggered along the path." Gans, *The Le Corbusier Guide* (New York: Princeton Architectural Press, 2006), p.61.

6.4 Interior of hall of 24 Rue Nungesser et Coli (1933).

6.5 Bottom of the stair in the lightwell of 24 Rue Nungesser et Coli (1933).

6.6 Gallery from which the penthouse is accessed, 24 Rue Nungesser et Coli (1933).

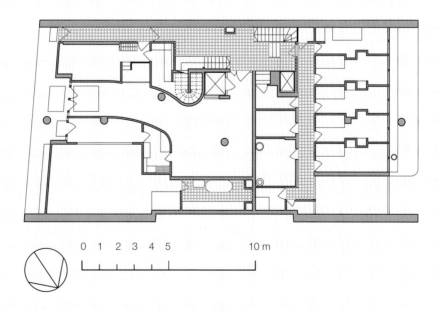

0 1 2 3 4 5   10 m

6.3 Plan at ground floor level of 24 Rue Nungesser et Coli (1933).

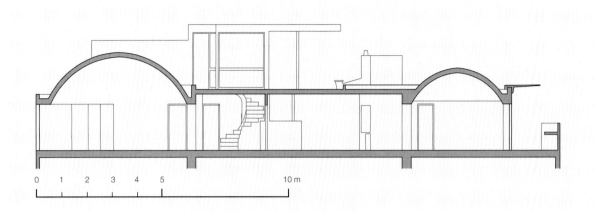

6.7 **Section across Penthouse, 24 Rue Nungesser et Coli (1933).**

Sensitising Vestibule

Like the Maison La Roche, the apartment is entered at the hinge of two very different zones, each celebrated with a vault, one devoted to Le Corbusier's own studio, the other to living and dining (Figs. 6.7 and 6.8). Each is hidden by a vast pivoting door. The side facing into the living room is black, the other side cream, as befits the spaces to which they are dedicated. The odd skewed wall in a deep blue that greets the reader upon entry encourages movement towards the living rooms as do the attractive qualities of the bright red fireplace beyond (Fig. 6.9). When open, the pivoting door into Le Corbusier's studio contributes to this funnelling of space which is further reinforced by the sweep of the side of the spiral staircase and transition zone created by the doorway of the living room.

Questioning – *savoir habiter*

Here the third stage of Le Corbusier's narrative arc, a space for questioning, is taken to new extremes. In chapter 4 I mentioned Le Corbusier's fondness for the split screen format used by the Renaissance painter Piero della Francesca (Fig. 4.5). This split screen is used in several of the photos of the penthouse in the *Œuvre Complète*, but the one that is particularly significant is a carefully choreographed view of the fireplace in the main living room which would be encountered immediately on entry into the apartment (Fig. 6.10). In this case two thirds of the image is devoted to the fireplace, whilst the final third is of Le Corbusier and Yvonne standing on the balcony beyond in a dialogue of then and now.

The foreground of the living room photo is occupied by a rectangular niche containing three very anthropomorphic "primitive" objects. They are on the same level as the figures of Yvonne and Le Corbusier and seem to be of the same stature. To the left of the niche, lit by the sun is a rotund pot, highly reminiscent of an ancient fertility goddess. She is in distinct contrast with the dark figure of Le Corbusier to the left of the balcony, yet she seems in some way connected to him, perhaps as an expression of his other side. The shady priapic statuette on the right appears to have a similar correspondence with the figure of Yvonne. The sunlight falling on the feminine pot evokes the Apollonian light of reason, while the darkness that falls on the little phallus is distinctly chthonic and feminine. Each object forms a tiny marriage of opposites by itself. Between them sits a block of black basalt, a play on the theme of the philosopher's stone. It seems no accident that they are surrounded in red, used by Le Corbusier as the colour of fusion in *Le Poème de l'angle droit*.

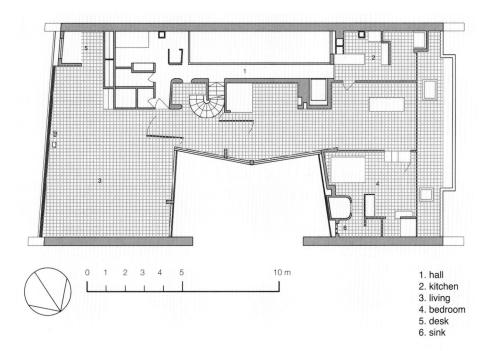

0 1 2 3 4 5   10 m

1. hall
2. kitchen
3. living
4. bedroom
5. desk
6. sink

6.8 **Plan of penthouse, 24 Rue Nungesser et Coli (1933).**

6.9 **View from studio, through hall to fireplace and dining space beyond of the Penthouse (1933).**

6.11 **Photograph of "Exhibition of Art So Called 'Primitive'" (1935) held in the Penthouse from the *Œuvre Complète*.**

6.12 **A painting by Le Corbusier, a statue by Laurens, a tapestry by Léger and other objects that evoke a poetic reaction in the "Exhibition of Art So Called 'Primitive'" (1935) held in the Penthouse from the *Œuvre Complète*.**

The union of opposites is reiterated in the orthogonal aperture of the black fireplace where feminine darkness is framed by a masculine geometry and in the black and white fur of the organic animal skin in front of it, which lies, in turn, on the cold industrial tiles of the floor.[8] Then we notice the contrast between these flat shiny tiles and the matt warmth of the shadowy round vaults of the ceiling above. Light and dark, vertical and horizontal, geometric and organic, the contrasts permeate Le Corbusier's work of this period. As Le Corbusier wrote of the Unité in Marseilles, "I will create beauty by contrast, I will find the opposite element, I will establish a dialogue between the rough and the finished, between precision and accident, between the lifeless and the intense and in this way I will encourage people to observe and reflect."[9] This then was one of the tactics used by Le Corbusier for the promotion of *savoir habiter* within the temple of his own family.

In 1935 in a peculiar blurring of public and private, an "Exhibition of Art So Called 'Primitive'" was held in the Nungesser et Coli penthouse.[10] Although ostensibly curated by Louis Carré, there is much of Le Corbusier in the layout of the pieces. The black and white photographs depicting the exhibition in the *Œuvre Complète* reveal much about the way Le Corbusier played with texture, colour and narrative to create overlaps across time as well as space. In Le Corbusier's studio a plaster cast of an early Greek statue of a man carrying a calf – colourfully painted by Le Corbusier – merges into the rough stone wall behind while its contours are echoed in the Aubusson Carpet that hangs upon the wall, a design by Fernand Léger (Fig. 6.11). "Full, empty, light, matter: a tapestry of Léger, a statue by Laurens."[11] In this photo (Fig. 6.12) the curved arm of Le Corbusier's painting is echoed by Laurens' statue and the Léger behind, as if part of the same composition.

In an echo of the fireplace photograph discussed earlier (Fig. 6.10) a bronze figurine from Benin sits atop a brick creating a diagonal slash of space from high to low that is itself echoed by the diagonal of light that washes

8   Pearson writes of Le Corbusier's habit of "superimposing organic forms over an organising grid". Pearson, "Integrations of Art and Architecture", p.312.

9   Ibid., p.190.

10   Le Corbusier and Pierre Jeanneret, *Œuvre Complète Volume 3, 1934–38* (Zurich: Les Editions d'Architecture, 1945), pp.156–157. Originally published in 1938.

11   Ibid., p.157.

6.10 **Carefully composed shot of living room of the Penthouse from the** *Œuvre Complète.*

6.13 **Another fireplace composition in the "Exhibition of Art So Called 'Primitive'" (1935) held in the Penthouse from the** *Œuvre Complète.*

across the frame, past a vast stone from a British beach, extending towards an ancient Greek statue of a woman (Fig. 6.13). It occupies the foreground, disturbing the delicate balance of near and far in this place. Games are played in the distribution of artefacts within Le Corbusier's own home, not only to alter our perception of space, but this time to collapse our sense of time – the many centuries that separate the ancient statue and that of Laurens, and of culture, the many miles travelled by the Benin figurine. The exhibition seems to encapsulate the belief, mentioned in chapter 4, that it is the job of the poet to transcend limitations of time.

Although a concrete-framed building with minimal non-load bearing partitions, the flat, described by Peter Carl as a "museum cave", feels anything but flimsy.[12] Close inspection of the thresholds between the key spaces reveals why this is the case. The frames of the vast doors, often surmounted by a shelf, are given a depth quite disproportionate to the lightweight walls that they inhabit, as they mark the points between

---

12   P. Carl, "Le Corbusier's Penthouse in Paris: 24 Rue Nungesser et Coli", *Daidalos*, 28 (1988), pp.65–75.

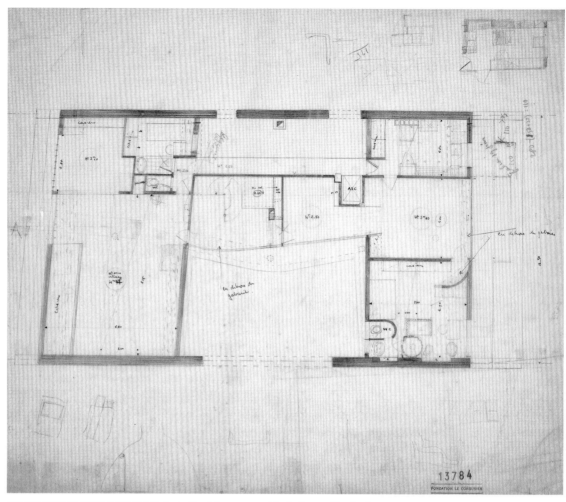

6.14 **Developmental plan of threshold between the dining space and the bedroom of the Penthouse
showing the introduction of a small lobby, FLC 13784.**

distinct zones of activity. The thresholds marking the ends of the vaults are particularly deep. Developmental drawings indicate that Le Corbusier wanted to find a way to give emphasis to one such threshold, that between the dining room and his and Yvonne's bedroom (Fig. 6.14).[13] However, the solution to this problem did not lie so much in plan as in section where manipulations at the high level of shelf, shadow, frame and vault give strong sensation of depth (Fig. 6.15). Nowadays a large wardrobe on rumbling castors swings round with maximum drama to create a door nearly a metre in girth. (Figs. 6.16 and 6.17)

In the deepest recesses of the bedroom itself is an alcove devoted to washing (6 on Fig. 6.8). Here the view is frustrated by a glass block window, the only view being that into the small circular mirror which Le Corbusier would look at himself while he shaved (Fig. 6.18). On the other side of the penthouse in the studio wing (Fig. 6.19), hidden by a wall of pigeonholes is Le Corbusier's own inner sanctum, the little desk where he wrote and thought (5 on Fig. 6.8). As at his sink, light pours in through the glass blocks but there is nothing to look at (Fig. 6.20). There are no easy answers or conspicuously framed views, only incitements to further introspection. The reader must therefore return to the spiral stair with which this account begins.

---

13   Fondation Le Corbusier (hereafter referred to as FLC) 13784 in H. Allen Brookes (ed.), *The Le Corbusier Archive, Volumes XI*, p.231. Hereafter referred to as
      Allen Brookes, *Archive XI*.

6.15 **Deep threshold in the Penthouse, Rue Nungesser et Coli (1933).**

6.16 **Wardrobe door into Le Corbusier's and Yvonne's bedroom, the Penthouse, 24 Rue Nungesser et Coli (1933).**

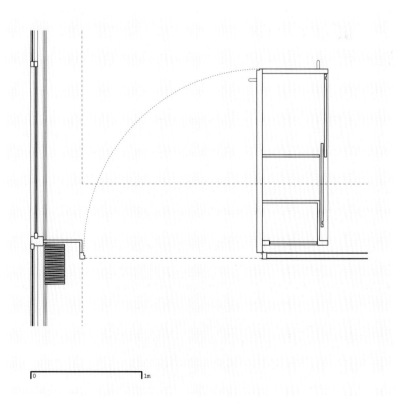

6.17 **Plan of the threshold between the dining room and Le Corbusier's and Yvonne's bedroom, the Penthouse, 24 Rue Nungesser et Coli (1933).**

6.20 **Le Corbusier at his desk in the Penthouse, 24 Rue Nungesser et Coli (1933).**

6.18 **Le Corbusier's shaving mirror in the Penthouse, Rue Nungesser et Coli (1933).**

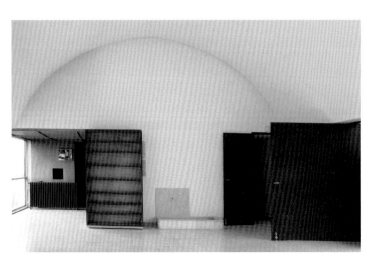

6.19 **Le Corbusier's studio in the Penthouse, 24 Rue Nungesser et Coli (1933). The alcove to the desk is to the left, the basin in the centre.**

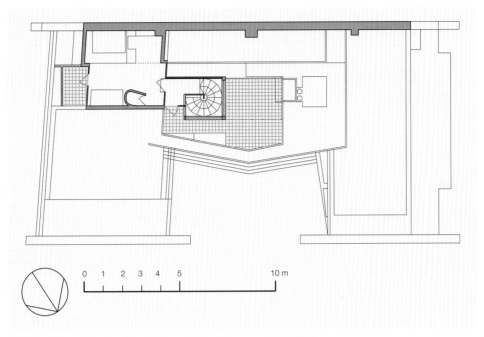

6.21 **Plan of the roof garden of the Penthouse, 24 Rue Nungesser et Coli (1933).**

Reorientation

Guarded by a series of "objects that provoke a poetic reaction" the spiral stair in the vestibule is painted black on its outer edges, but its treads are light, illuminated from above. The circle of the stair contrasts with the square space within which it sits, again in a play of opposites – the special qualities of each form felt most strongly when set against the other (Fig. 6.21). It has no guard rail, just a simple pole at the centre of the spiral, meaning that it has much of the quality of one of Le Corbusier's precarious stairs, designed to awaken a consciousness of space and of danger (Fig. 6.22) giving access to the spare bedroom and the tiny roof garden above (Fig. 6.22).

Culmination

In the photos in the *Œuvre Complète*, emphasis is placed upon the view across the lantern to the roof garden, which itself acts as a frame for views of the sky, but there is a conspicuous lack of climax to the route, beyond the overwhelming sensation of light and space that occurs in any rooftop haven. The view instead is bounced back into the boundaries of the little, seemingly square, garden contributing strongly to the hermetic sense of the whole.[14](Fig. 6.23)

The penthouse at 24 Rue Nungesser et Coli was built at a point of transition in Le Corbusier's architecture between the "white" buildings of his early career and the later more brutalist work. It also marks a transition in his thinking on the promenade, heralding a tendency that would reach its most extreme expression in La Tourette, in which the aim is to create continuity with the inner world of the people who live there. The penthouse is entered upon a hinge. From here two equal but opposing routes can be accessed, one through the living space and one through the studio, each given a staccato rhythm by the beams of the

14   See for an expansion of this discussion Flora Samuel, "Le Corbusier, Women, Nature and Culture", *Issues in Art and Architecture*, 5, 2 (1998), pp.1–17.

6.22 **Staircase up to roof garden of the Penthouse, 24 Rue Nungesser et Coli (1933).**

6.23 **The roof garden of the Penthouse, 24 Rue Nungesser et Coli (1933).**

vaults overhead. Both come to a dead end, forcing the reader back to the entrance hall where he or she began. The culminating route up the spiral stair to the roof garden lacks the focus of the Villa Savoye and offers limited possibilities of release.

Summary

Le Corbusier thought of himself as a monk, Père Corbu, living with the spiritual torment and anguish that he believed to be the key elements of monastic existence, but without the intolerable constraints of celibacy. The promenade of the penthouse at 24 Rue Nungesser et Coli follows the five-part narrative up to a point, its rhetoric seemingly directed at his wife Yvonne who preferred her old home, 23 Rue Jacob. Here, as will be seen in La Tourette and indeed *Le Poème de l'angle droit* – which is, after all about his relationship with his wife – the drama is internalised, cyclical and has no easy ending. Perhaps ironically Yvonne ended her days a near prisoner as, being lame in the extreme, she was unable to climb down the stairs to the outer world, unable or unwilling to appreciate the promenade Le Corbusier had intended. Late in life Le Corbusier acknowledged this, reflecting with deep regret that he had "kept her in a box".[15]

15   Jane Drew interviewed by Margaret Garlake, 20–21 May 1995, National Life Story Collection, British Library, F823.

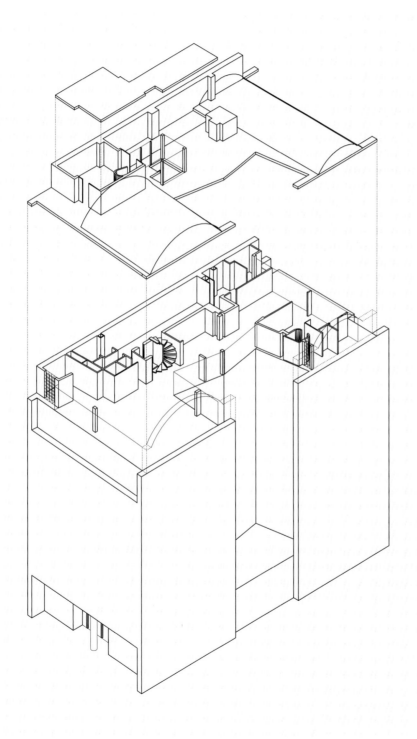

6.24 **Isometric drawing showing elements of the architectural promenade of the Penthouse, 24 Rue Nungesser et Coli (1933).**

MAISON JAOUL B 1955–57

The Maisons Jaoul are a complex of two vaulted houses, designed for the steel industrialist Michel Jaoul in the early 1950s in, then suburban, Neuilly on the outskirts of Paris. As at the Villa Savoye "the aspect of the sun dominated the lay-out of the plans and sections".[16] House A, designed for the father, is parallel to the street with House B, designed for the son, shielded behind. It is the rather more relaxed spaces of Maison B that are to be read here (Fig. 6.25). The house receives extensive treatment in Caroline Maniaque's excellent book *Le Corbusier and the Maisons Jaoul* which illustrates the multiplicity of interpretations latent in a single building. She devotes a chapter to the "promenade" but its elements are not addressed in any great detail.

Both houses are structured around two parallel lines of catalan vaults, one wide and one narrow. These give a strict discipline to the development of the façade (Fig. 6.26) and govern the direction of the promenade. The larger 2/3 of the section is given to the main spaces, the remaining 1/3 to ancillary spaces, kitchens, children's rooms and so on. Again it is necessary to recall Le Corbusier's fondness for the tripartite division of Renaissance paintings as there is a certain tension between near and far which acts as an enticement to entry. Where the promenade is in the direction of the vault all space is compelling space, driven on by the lines of the vast beams that power ever onward. The task here is to contain the forward thrust. Le Corbusier wrote, "the designing of such a house demanded extreme care since the elements of construction were the only architectonic means".[17]

Generally walls carry the load from vaults but, in the case of the Maisons Jaoul there are massive concrete lintels which distribute the load of the vaults across the varied openings in the huge spine walls that divide the cross section.[18] As Le Corbusier stated, "the composition consists of opening holes in these parallel walls and playing the solid/open game, but playing intensely the architectural game".[19] To this end the linear spaces are segmented transversally, each slice giving form to the next stage in the journey. (Fig. 6.27)

"The elements are the construction parti (idea or system), the choice of materials", wrote Le Corbusier. These are "the most rudimentary, the most everyday",[20] brick, tile and catalan vaults with grass roofs. A very important touchstone for this building is art, the "primitive" art of Dubuffet, of which Jaoul owned a large collection. The characteristic of Dubuffet's often stark and shocking creations is a raw sensory appeal, an extreme tactility which carries some deep inner message. The three things seem to be fundamental to Maison Jaoul B which for Le Corbusier represented a "bringing into focus" – mise au point – "of the constituent elements of architecture to be understood"[21], in this way alerting us to the moralising or didactic function of the building.

---

16   Le Corbusier, *Œuvre Complète Volume 5, 1946–1952* (Zurich: Les Editions d'Architecture, 1973), p.173. Originally published in 1953.
17   Le Corbusier and Pierre Jeanneret, *Œuvre Complète Volume 3*, p.125.
18   See for an account of the development of these vaults C. Maniaque, *Le Corbusier et les Maisons Jaoul* (Paris: Picard, 2005), pp.84–87.
19   Le Corbusier, *Œuvre Complète Volume 5*, p.173.
20   Ibid., p.216.
21   Le Corbusier, *Œuvre Complète Volume 6, 1952–1957* (Zurich: Les Editions d'Architecture, 1985), p.208. Originally published in 1957.

6.25 **The Maisons Jaoul view from the ramp from the *Œuvre Complète* (1955–57).**

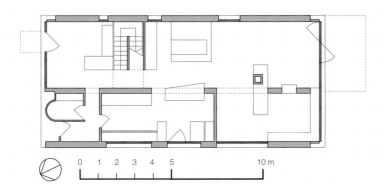

0 1 2 3 4 5   10 m

6.26 **Ground floor plan of Maison Jaoul B (1955–57).**

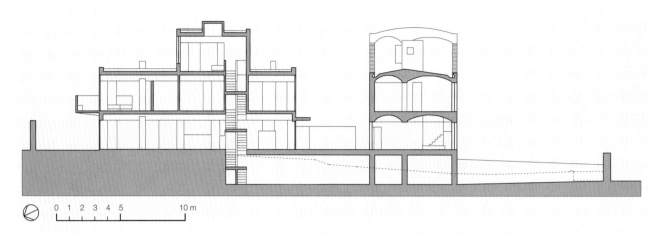

6.27 **Section across Maison Jaoul B (1955–57).**

Threshold

The gate on Rue de Longchamp provides the first element to be negotiated en route into the house. At street level access is provided up to the house and down to the underworld of the car park by a pair of ramps working in counterpoint to one another. Up three steps the reader arrives at a square courtyard finished in large square slabs that make it appear smaller than it really is. As in the triple height space of the Maison La Roche or the hallway in 24 Rue Nungesser et Coli the courtyard acts as the hinge between the two homes. The doorway of house A is parallel with the ramp, the doorway to house B faces on to it on one side, shadowed by a large horizontal concrete awning which is very simple with a spout to the side (Fig. 6.28). Above it the long concrete lintel overshadowing the timber panelling adds a further depth to the threshold, as does a thin plinth at ground level. So although the door itself is extremely simple in elevation, it is set into a highly complex and layered façade.

Sensitising Vestibule

The two exterior faces of the vestibule are timber-panelled window walls with shutters at high and low levels. The vestibule is as usual square in plan. It feels in one way highly enclosed, hemmed in by the dark spine wall of the staircase. In another way it is totally open to the enfilade vista across the house and to the staircase winding above. Already the reader has been alerted to the strange spatial games that are such a characteristic of this house.

Beneath the stair a seat, a slab of timber of gargantuan girth provides a place to sit and take off shoes (Fig. 6.29). Beside it a polished concrete altar of a table receives the visitor's keys and bag. Entry to the building is accompanied by a tiny uterine bathroom tucked away in the minor bay of the building, but expressed voluptuously in brick curves on its exterior. Cleansing and rebirth are celebrated here as at the Villa Savoye. Embedded in the floor is one tile painted by Le Corbusier "only wash this floor with spirits of sel/sol" – salt or sun, the reading is ambiguous, simultaneously evocative of washing-up adverts and paganism (Fig. 6.30).

Questioning – *savoir habiter*

Rowe writes of the balance of orthogonal and transverse movement that characterises Corbusian space. Nowhere is this felt more strongly than at the base of the stairs of Maison B where tensions between upward, onward and sideways movement beset the reader who receives no clues from the uniform cream tiles of the floor, but is ultimately drawn on by the promise of light into the questioning part of the narrative, the salon

6.28 **Door into Maison Jaoul B (1955–57) from the *Œuvre Complète*.**

6.29 **Hallway of Maison Jaoul B (1955–57).**

6.30 **Tile in the floor of Maison Jaoul B (1955–57).**

6.32 **Diagram showing implied squares of key spaces in the ground floor of Maison Jaoul B (1955–57) as well as an area of spatial overlap between the dining and living spaces.**

6.33 **Rear of fireplace in Maison Jaoul B (1955–57).**

6.31 **Salon of Maison Jaoul B (1955–57) towards stairwell.**

(Fig. 6.31). Here there is a square zone for a dining table which is actually part of a larger rectangular space which itself is part of a larger square (Fig. 6.32). As Gyorgy Kepes writes of modernist art in 1944, "space not only recedes but fluctuates in a continuous activity".[22] An odd overlapping experience of space is brought into existence, the equivalent in plan of what is happening on the façade.

At the heart of the composition is a highly sculptural fireplace. Yet this is no fireplace, just a painting of fire both tantalising and teasing (Fig. 6.33). The real fire can be found in the hearth on the other side, forcing an about-turn in the direction of the route (Fig. 6. 34). This fireside space, like the hall at the other end of the build-ing, is square in plan giving it a certain peaceful demeanour. It is a place to stop and think. Distractions are minimal, just the little study space to the side which would presumably have provided a home for Jaoul's artworks as an object of contemplation. Indeed there is such a sense of repose that there is little incitement to return back along the building and climb the stair, apart from a glimpse of landing behind the sideboard which acts like a gesturing finger through a screen calling us up, at once beckoning and suggestive.[23]

---

22   Gyorgy Kepes, *Language of Vision* (Chicago, 1944), p.77 quoted in Colin Rowe and Robert Slutsky, "Transparency: Literal and Phenomenal" in Colin Rowe, *The Mathematics of the Ideal Villa* (Cambridge MA: MIT, 1976), p.161.
23   Ibid., p.222.

6.34 **Fireplace of Maison Jaoul B (1955–57).**

6.36 **Green flue at the end of the corridor on the first floor of Maison Jaoul B (1955–57).**

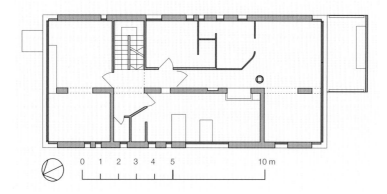

6.35 **Plan of first floor of Maison Jaoul B (1955–57).**

6.37 **Ladder in side wall of stairwell up to second floor of Maison Jaoul B (1955–57).**

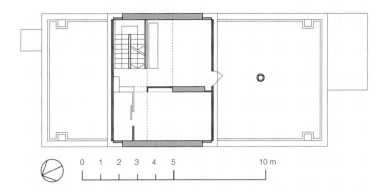

6.38 **Plan of second floor of Maison Jaoul B (1955–57).**

Reorientation

The sequence of images of Jaoul B in the *Œuvre Complète* leads across into the living space and then back up to the stair. Here are three photos of the stair from different angles, emphasising its role as the core point of reorientation of the narrative, "part of a plastic architectural game".[24] As is common with Le Corbusier, the treads of this stair are cantilevered off the central wall of the dogleg, leaving a gap at the side of the treads which renders them slightly unnerving, a trick of gravity, a leap of faith. The walls that give structural support to the treads are painted black to diminish their importance whereas the walls that very clearly do not support the stair are painted white, exaggerating the sleight of hand that has gone into supporting this stair from the central wall and to reinforce the effect of the light pouring through the gaps at its edges. The rail on the first flight is of white ribbon steel, very insubstantial, cold and not that pleasant to touch, wakening again the senses of the hand.

The corridor at first floor (Fig. 6.35) is on the central axis of the building, but the view through the master bedroom and out to the garden beyond is impeded by the flue of the chimney from the fire below that blocks the view through. It is painted green (Fig. 6.36). The same green is used on one side of the concrete beam and wall by the stairwell. This has the effect of foreshortening the rather relentless space as the green elements appear to coalesce together, a common Corbusian trick.

Arriving at the first floor landing the reader is pulled to the left, not to the right, which, lacking a fireplace flue, does not provide such a strong focus within the overall composition. To reach the bedroom it is necessary to squeeze between the column and the curved shower space in order to burst out into the contrasting orthogonality of the room. Turning against the light, the reader is then confronted by the red and blue pipes of the shower cubicle, like arteries, the inner waterworks of this home set against earthy brown tile, almost indecently organic. This space forms another caesura, walled in by the green column and the enveloping curves, but the reader is driven onwards by the memory of light on the stairwell which provides a continuing impetus upwards.

Standing on the first floor landing at the bottom of the next flight of stairs a steel ladder, of the sort more usually used to access a signal box or a crane, can be seen set into the side wall of the house above (Fig. 6.37). To heave yourself up the ladder, which takes a certain amount of physical exertion, is to feel that you have

---

6.39 **View down stair from second floor of Maison Jaoul B (1955–57).**

been tricked. True, it does allow you to pop your head above the mullion of the window and to see the road beyond along the length of the two houses, but it does little else beyond making you wonder why you were so easily distracted.

Clambering back down the reader continues to the airy studio that tops the house. The stair it transpires has been lit by a side light that penetrates upwards beyond the confines of the vault above. It suggests the possibilities of a further journey into the sky, one where we cannot go. The stairwell is not, in reality, contained within high walls as it is in the plans in the *Œuvre Complète*, meaning that the spaces bleed into one another, giving a strong sense of expansion at the top of the stairwell (Fig. 6.38).

Here set within the angle of the solid balustrade appears a little seat which again is not found in the *Œuvre Complète*. Its function is to provide a place of recovery after the exertions of climbing the stairs. Le Corbusier's buildings are designed for the encouragement of athleticism, an awareness of the pull of muscles, physical release, and the beating of the heart. Slightly unresolved, the seat is one of those odd remnants that invites input from the reader – its potential as a play space and eyrie is unlimited as it offers a vertical drop to the floor below. The blank walls and relative darkness of this corner mean that our attention turns in the opposite direction, in the direction in which memories of the building below have already programmed the reader's footsteps.

Culmination

It takes only a few steps to reach the window on the far side of the room which is deeply framed like a door. Once it is opened there is a step up and over onto a wide wooden shelf to a Virgilian garden, within which rises the flue from below, now painted white, swathed in a field of grass and irises like a lone column in a ruinous landscape (Fig. 6.40).

6.40 **View out of door onto roof of Maison Jaoul B (1955–57).**

Intensely picturesque, Le Corbusier's Romantic roots come to a pitch here. In a sense the house has petered out into the sky, a reverie on time, death and dissolution. Just like the vaulted pisé houses of La Sainte Baume, the vaults of Jaoul B provide a glimpse of life underground, the cave of the Magdalene across the valley floor, where she lived half in life half in death only sustained by the music of angels. Like Jaoul B, these elemental houses, intensely ascetic, were built to encourage reflection and hermitage in sociable circumstances.

Summary

The Maison Jaoul B marks a return to the certainties of the Jacob's ladder route expressed so clearly in the Villa Savoye. Le Corbusier uses layers and extremely raw materials, rather than a tortuous variation on the usual promenade format, to heighten the reader's awareness of both space and time. The promenade is clear, up the stairs and into the lofty roofspace and out the door to the sky (Fig. 6.41).

Conclusion

Overhead vaults profoundly affect the character of the promenade. The presence of the transverse vaults in the Penthouse cuts up the promenade and prohibits the creation of the kind of ambiguous overlapping volumes that is such a characteristic of Maison Jaoul, both in plan and elevation.

To enter a volume that one moment feels like a square and the next moment feels like a corner of a larger volume gives a flickering quality to the experience which encourages the reader onwards. The transition expressed by these examples is not just that between the early white architecture and something more colourful and textured, it is a transition between two different ways of conceiving space, the first as a series of planes, the second as a series of overlapping volumes.

The stages of the narrative path are extremely clear in Maison Jaoul B, much less so at 24 Rue Nungesser et Coli. It is a very different thing to design a house for someone else than to design a home for yourself. The architect must put on a performance, be persuasive and full of certainty to win the confidence of the client. He or she must also categorise and make assessments, often based upon stereotypical assumptions, of what might be needed. The result may be tidy, but with little basis in the reality of the client's needs. This, I believe, is why the promenades in houses built for clients are so much more clearly articulated than that within Le Corbusier's own home which is instead more inconclusive – more expressive of the complexities and doubts of his own existence.

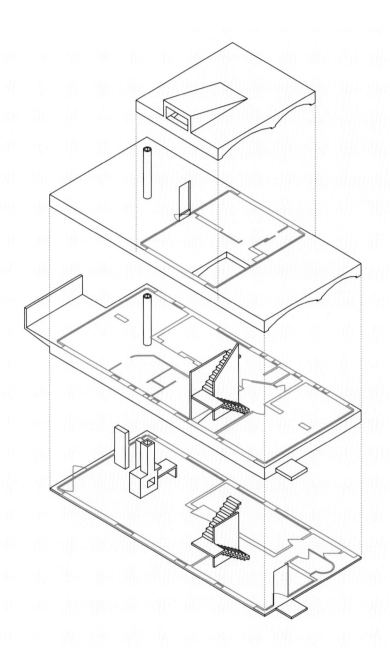

6.41 **Isometric showing the elements of the architectural promenade in Maison Jaoul B (1955–57).**

7.1 **The main second floor factory space of Usine Duval (1946–51).**

That Le Corbusier's domestic work largely conformed to what I have called his five-part narrative path should now be clear. What I want to demonstrate in this chapter is how that narrative structure was changed and distorted in his more public buildings, those with complex multiple routes and a variety of possible readings. Three case studies have been chosen, each with a very different take on the basic Jacob's ladder format. In the Usine Duval the idealistic Jacob's ladder type promenade works in opposition to the practicalities of factory production. The ground floor of the Maison du Brésil provides an internal travelogue of Le Corbusier's idealised vision of that country, while in La Tourette the real world promenade is truncated in favour of an otherworldly climax within the cosmic spaces of the Soul.

USINE DUVAL 1946–51

Factory production appealed to Le Corbusier's spirit of orderliness.[1] He was overwhelmed by a visit to the Ford Factory at Detroit where "everyone works to one end, all are in agreement, all have the same objective and all their thoughts and actions flow along the same channel".[2] The Usine Duval, the only factory ever built by Le Corbusier, illustrates the tensions between functionalism – the most efficient transportation of things around the building – and the route of initiation.

This concrete structure, a reconstruction of a millinery factory owned by Jean-Jacques Duval, which had been destroyed in World War II, retains the memory of its former incarnation in the rubble of the side walls. An "entirely Modulor'" building,[3] the Usine (Fig. 7.1) is linked by Le Corbusier with the Unité in Marseilles that dates from the previous year, 1945. "Both express a rude health, their colour schemes being pushed to a most powerful intensity." The emphasis here is upon harmony "in a game of a subtlety almost musical".[4] This is a building that acts upon the body through rhythm and colour, an initiation into the powers of harmony, like that of La Sainte Baume, that follows on from it in the pages of the *Œuvre Complète*.

For Le Corbusier the radiant use of number was a key aspect of the process of unification. Indeed the Usine Duval must be seen against a backdrop of Le Corbusier's ideas from the *Radiant City* in which work and life would be balanced within a society built upon mutual respect, not money, hence the significance of Le Corbusier's symbol of the Open Hand – celebrated in section F of *Le Poème de l'angle droit* – to this particular scheme.

1   Le Corbusier and Pierre Jeanneret, *Œuvre Complète Volume 1, 1910–1929* (Zurich: Girsberger, 1943), p.78. Originally published in 1937.
2   Le Corbusier and Pierre Jeanneret, *Œuvre Complète Volume 3, 1934–38* (Zurich: Les Editions d'Architecture, 1995), p.24. Originally published in 1938.
3   Le Corbusier, *Œuvre Complète Volume 5, 1946–1952* (Zurich: Les Editions d'Architecture, 1995), p.13. Originally published in 1953.
4   Ibid., p.14.

7.2 **Section across Usine Duval (1946–51).**

It is open because
All is present available
Knowable
Open to receive
Open also that others
Might come and take…
Full hand I received
Full hand I now give.[5]

Le Corbusier's description of the Van Nelle Factory in Rotterdam, first published in one of the syndicalist journals that he wrote for in the early 1930s and later reprinted in *The Radiant City*, gives a strong indication that he saw collective production as a spiritual quest.

The Van Nelle tobacco factory in Rotterdam, a creation of the modern age, has removed all the former connotation of despair from that word "proletarian." And this deflection of the egoistic property instinct towards a feeling for collective action leads to a most happy result: the phenomenon of personal participation in every stage of the human enterprise. Labour retains its fundamental materiality, but it is enlightened by the spirit. I repeat, everything lies in that phrase: *a proof of love*.

It is to this goal, by means of the new administrative forms that will purify and amplify it, that we must lead our modern world. Tell us what we are, what we can do to help, why we are working… *Unite us*. Speak to us. Are we not all one, within the *serene* whole of an organised hierarchy?

If you show us such plans and explain them to us, the old dichotomy between "haves" and despairing "have-nots" will disappear. There will be but a single society, united in belief and action.

We live in an age of strictest rationalism, and this is a matter of conscience. We must awaken a conscience in the world. Conscience in everyone and about everyone.

It is a spiritual task.

The noblest of tasks also, and the only one that excites, or can excite, a passionate response in everyone. It is the truest task of mankind; its reason for being.

Spiritual satisfaction, spiritual joy – individually and collectively at the same time… The play is already well under way: the misers, the traitors and the cowards are already on the stage; but so too are the debonair knights, assured of ultimate victory.[6]

5   Le Corbusier, *Le Poème de l'angle droit* (Paris: Editions Connivance, 1989), section F3, Offering.
6   Le Corbusier, *The Radiant City* (London, Faber, 1967, p.177. Originally published as *La Ville Radieuse* (Paris: Editions de l'Architecture d'Aujourd'hui, 1935).

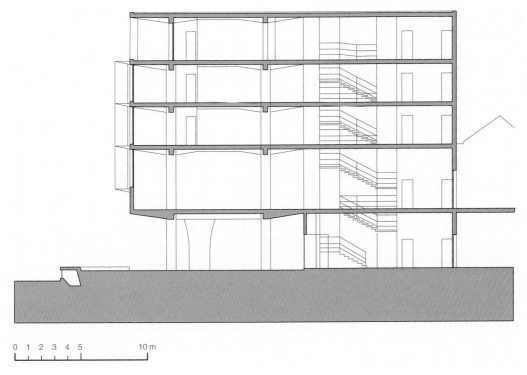

0 1 2 3 4 5   10 m

7.3 **Section across Usine Duval (1946–51).**

Le Corbusier echoes the statement "we must awaken a conscience in the world" in the St Dié correspondence, indicating the extent that the Usine Duval was predicated on this vision.[7] The idea here was to promote the understanding of *savoir habiter* by creating a stimulating workplace environment. This then is the central concern of the scheme.[8]

Threshold

As with most piloti buildings the actual extent and entry of the Usine Duval is very ambiguous, allowing the building and its surroundings to blur together (Fig. 7.2). On the street a little concrete portal set into a chain-link fence marks the point of entry. From here it is necessary to step up onto the plinth beneath the building the soffit of which painted in bright polychrome colours (Fig. 7.3).

The double doors giving access to both factory and offices are extremely simple, set into a glazed frame so that the barrier between interior and exterior is minimised. The stone of the floor slabs passes from within to without, further blurring the distinction between the two. A relief sculpture of the Open Hand is set into the wall next to it, setting the agenda of the factory, the giving and receiving of love.

Sensitising Vestibule

The entrance hall, an implied square as is usual in Le Corbusier's buildings, is linked to a series of spaces built from the remnants of what existed on the site before (Fig. 7.4).[9] The chamfered receptionist's table at ground level inflects the reader towards a fiercely white service core that gives access to each of the three

7   Daniel Grandidier, *Le Corbusier et St. Dié* (St Dié: Musée Municipal, 1987), p.115.
8   See letter Le Corbusier to Raoul Dautry, 21 Dec. 1945 reprinted in ibid., p.60.
9   Daniel Grandidier, *Le Corbusier et St. Dié*, 1987), p.115.

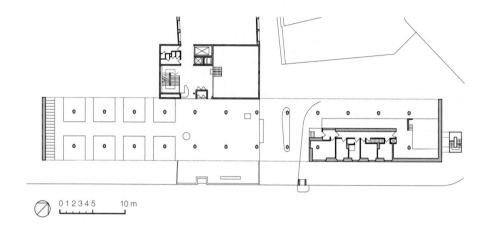

0 1 2 3 4 5   10 m

7.4 **Plan at ground level of Usine Duval (1946–51).**

7.6 **Top of main stairwell at office level of Usine Duval (1946–51).**

7.5 **Main stairwell at Usine Duval (1946–51).**

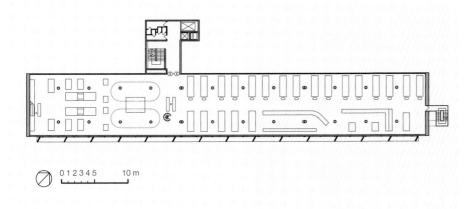

012345   10 m

7.8 **Plan at second floor level of Usine Duval (1946–51).**

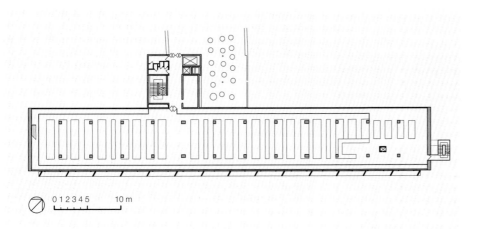

012345   10 m

7.7 **Plan at first floor level of Usine Duval (1946–51).**

levels of the factory, offering views out over the landscape at every level, so enabling the employees to "see clearly" the requirements of the task. This practical stairway serves as the key circulation route through the building (Fig. 7.5). It is egalitarian with no change in detail as it swerves up past the factory floors to the managers' offices above. The metal handrails and balustrades are minimal in the extreme. When ceiling heights dictate it, the stair hangs in space like a bridge before continuing up to the next floor. Upon arrival at the offices, the reader is greeted yet again by a vast relief of the symbol of the Open Hand, reinforcing once more the central message of the building (Fig. 7.6).

Questioning – *savoir habiter*

The process of making begins with pattern cutting in the topmost gallery space of the factory. From here hats and other artefacts travel down the building, according to their stage of evolution, on a rather theatrical set of slides and chutes to the storage floor at first floor level from which they are dispatched on lorries (Fig. 7.7). The production line here works counter to the upward momentum of the Jacob's ladder. The operatives themselves have specialist tasks in the production process and feed into the different floors according to where their skills are needed. The main promenade appears to be directed at the managers in the offices on the topmost floor whose job according to Le Corbusier was to think and to lead.

7.9 **Spiral stairway from second floor of Usine Duval (1946–51).**

Access to the galleried spaces of the main factory floor is provided at second floor level (Fig. 7.8) through a thick threshold that negotiates between the upward thrust of the stair and the horizontality of the space of production. Pilotis march across the factory floor subdividing the activities within, linked above by rough cast concrete beams that are splayed at each end in rationalist emulation of the forces within them. These work with the lines of the fenestration and the painted coloured panels of the ceiling to create a friendly web of influence upon the operatives beneath. Yellow and red dominate here, spirit and body, interspersed by the green of the ventilation ducts which weave through the mix. At either end of the factory the rough stone walls of the exterior can be felt, very much as they can be felt at 24 Rue Nungesser et Coli, contrasting with the girders and pipes of the process held within, bringing to relief once again a consciousness of past and present.

Reorientation

The main point of reorientation, both symbolic and literal, within the cavernous space of the factory itself is provided by the extremely theatrical spiral stair that travels from second floor up to the offices. Here a dark drum rather like a huge silo opens up to reveal its yellow core and the delicate steel spiral within (Fig. 7.9). In Le Corbusier's writings there is frequent slippage between the word light and the word knowledge, the yellow here designating the seeping down of both from the upper floor. The rather ceremonial door, whilst keeping out noise, acts as a point of transition between the factory floor, the galleried floor above (Fig. 7.10) and the offices where the stair penetrates the floor of the clerestory-lit upper world . Emerging into the sunny waiting room at the top of the stair the reader is greeted yet again by the Open Hand and a reception desk with a direct view to the enfilade of offices beyond (Fig. 7.11).

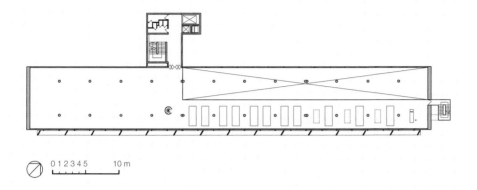

7.10 **Plan at third floor level of Usine Duval (1946–51).**

7.11 **Spiral staircase emerges into the office floor of Usine Duval (1946–51).**

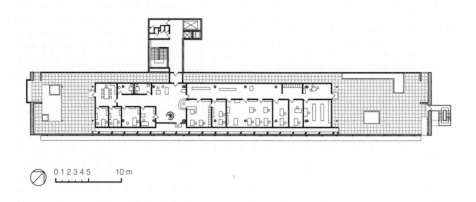

0 1 2 3 4 5   10 m

7.12 **Plan of office floor of Usine Duval (1946–51).**

Culmination

Whilst the office floor might be relatively straightforward in plan, the ceiling is strongly articulated – sometimes curved, sometimes fanning out from a column, in a manner reminiscent of a Gothic cathedral. Details from Le Corbusier's paintings have been wallpapered to the walls, blown up vastly distorting the scale and texture of the space, one in each of the managers' offices, a reminder of the true cause of this enterprise. Sometimes the doors themselves are papered in these images, meaning that it is necessary to negotiate with the image and its meaning in order to pass through the door. With the bright panels of colour, the vast murals and the shifting ceiling a full panoply of Corbusian techniques are marshalled together to bring the issue of space to the forefront (Fig. 7.13).

Le Corbusier mused frequently on the subject of intellectual leadership, believing that leaders had a very special role in passing knowledge down to those with less aptitude for understanding.[10] At the end of the enfilade of offices a single large meeting room, almost at the end of the promenade, is the nerve centre of the building. In this room the collective minds of the managers are focussed inward back onto the spiritual business of running a factory. From here a dramatic pivoting window gives access out on the rooftop garden and a final framed view of mountains beyond. The wall in which it sits is studded with an inlay of coloured tile – yellow, blue and green – used symbolically here to denote the classic Corbusian mantra of sun, space and greenery. This is the more spiritual climax of the promenade, occurring at the diametrically opposite end of the building from which hats, clothes and other products of the factory disappear into trucks to be sold.

10   For further discussion of this issue see Flora Samuel, "Le Corbusier, Teilhard de Chardin and La Planétisation humaine: spiritual ideas at the heart of modernism", *French Cultural Studies*, 11, 2 (2000), pp.181–200.

7.13 **View towards the manager's meeting room Usine Duval (1946–51).**

Summary

The basic elements of Le Corbusier's narrative path can be unearthed within the journey of the managers up through the shop floor against the tide of the factory process, through the spiral stair, up to the offices and out into nature (Fig. 7.14). Simultaneously the building accommodates sub-routes that muddy or enrich the promenade according to your point of view. These are the routes of the operatives moving towards the workstations in various parts of the factory. There is no denying that, however inviting Le Corbusier might make the route up to the offices or however egalitarian the detail of the main stair might be, the act of placing the managers on top of the pile is deeply hierarchical. The Usine Duval is a tremendously idealistic building pitting commercialism against co-operation, the material against the spiritual, expressed through the traffic of people and things around the building. In some ways it is however deeply flawed, representing in spatial terms the contradictions at the heart of Le Corbusier's egalitarian vision.

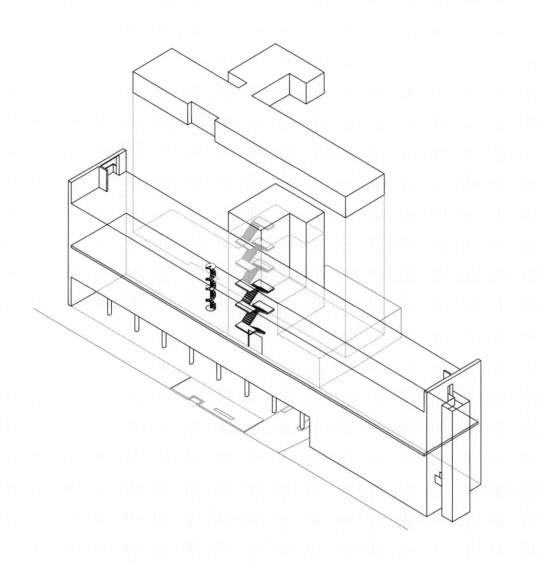

7.14 **Isometric showing the elements of the architectural promenade in the Usine Duval (1946–51).**

7.15 **Clouds in the partitions of the vestibule of the Maison du Brésil (1957–59).**

MAISON DU BRÉSIL 1957–59

This student housing block in the parkland setting of the Cité Universitaire in Paris was initially designed by the Rio architect Lucio Costa, but the final project, including the layout of the ground floor to be discussed here, was carried out by Le Corbusier's staff.[11] As if floating upon water, or standing in a lagoon, the entrance of the Maison du Brésil[12] sits on a plane of rippling black slate, laid in waves to Modulor proportions – what Le Corbusier called *opus optimum* – moving almost seamlessly from exterior to interior – for in Le Corbusier's work "the outside is always an inside".[13] The reader enters into the narrative as soon as he or she steps onto this heaving surface. It is a travelogue of Le Corbusier's experiences of Brazil, a story of elemental geography and flight like the novels of his friend Antoine de Saint Exupéry.[14] Here "everything rises; islands piercing the water, peaks falling into it, high hills and great mountains".[15] The tumult of impressions provided by such a landscape is captured wonderfully by Giuliana Bruno in relation to the picturesque garden:

A memory theatre of sensual pleasures, the garden was an exterior that put the spectator in touch with inner space. As one moved through the space of the garden, a constant double movement connected external to internal topographies. The garden was thus an outside turned into an inside, but it was also the projection of an inner world onto the outer geography. In a sensuous mobilisation, the exterior of the landscape was transformed into an interior map – the landscape within us – as this inner map was itself culturally mobilized. In this "moving" way, we came to approach the kind of transport that drives the architectonics of film spectatorship and of museum going.[16]

Her words strongly evoke the experience of the Maison du Brésil, a place where external and internal worlds collide.

Threshold

The Maison du Brésil is at a confluence of routes, one a road extending from the centre of the Cité Universitaire which swerves into the building carving out the space of the forecourt with its trajectory (Fig. 7.16). The second is a path from the large boulevard beyond, which curves towards the door of the Director's apartment (Fig. 7.17). The routes cross in the semicircle of space that prefaces the entrance itself (Fig. 7.18). Approaching from the heart of the Cité Universitaire, the reader walks at an oblique angle beneath the body of the building. Enclosure is here provided by a highly sculptural staircase (Fig. 7.19) pierced with planes of rough glass which gives an aqueous cast to the space below (Fig. 7.20). These appear exactly at the point where the hard surface of the street translates into the shining slate that extends into the building, together heralding a narrative of water.

---

11   Le Corbusier, *Œuvre Complète Volume 6, 1952–1957* (Zurich: Les Editions d'Architecture, 1985), p.202. Originally published in 1957.

12   The initial design was prepared by Lucio Costa, but documentary evidence suggests that Le Corbusier was decisive in his influence. See Cecília Rodrigues dos Santos, Margareth Campos da Silva Pereira, Romão Veriano da Silva Pereira, Vasco Caldeira da Silva, *Le Corbusier eo Brasil* (São Paulo: Projecto Editora, 1987), pp.244–301.

13   Le Corbusier, *Précisions* (Cambridge MA: MIT, 1991), p.78. Originally published as *Précisions sur un état présent de l'architecture et de l'urbanisme* (Paris: Crès, 1930).

14   See for example Antoine de Saint Exupéry, *Vol de nuit* (Paris: Editions Gallimard, 1931).

15   Le Corbusier, *Precisions*, p.2. For a discussion of the relationship of architecture and tourism see Stanislaus von Moos, "Voyages en Zigzag" in Stanislaus von Moos and Arthur Rüegg (eds.), *Le Corbusier Before Le Corbusier* (Yale: New Haven, 2002), pp.23–53.

16   Giuliana Bruno, *Public Intimacy: Architecture and the Visual Arts* (Cambridge MA: MIT, 2007), p.25.

7.16 **Route from the heart of the Cité Universitaire to the Maison du Brésil (1957–59).**

7.17 **Path spiralling in towards the entrance of the Director's apartment of the Maison du Brésil (1957–59).**

0 1 2 3 4 5   10 m

7.18 **Ground floor plan of the Maison du Brésil (1957–59).**

7.19 **Staircase of the Maison du Brésil (1957–59).**

7.20 **Panel of glass in staircase of the Maison du Brésil (1957–59).**

Sensitising Vestibule

In an early plan in the *Œuvre Complète* the little lobby that marks the point of entry to the Maison du Brésil is represented very emphatically as two walls that together halt the impetus of the route. However, as built, the vestibule sits only marginally proud of the taut plane of surrounding ondulatoire glazing within which it is set (Figs. 7.21 and 7.22). Positioned neatly between two pilotis it is overshadowed by the vast linear bulk of the building above. Together these gestures give it a certain authority. That this was the intention is evident from a number of design sketches.[17] Just before the door is a metal grating matwell, exactly the dimensions of the cube itself, making it look as though one defensive side of the box has folded down like a drawbridge to allow entry, amplifying the sensation that the reader is in some sense walking on water (Fig. 7.23).

The walls and ceilings of the cube are of glass fixed together with the most rudimentary of metal angles into the surrounding concrete structure (Fig. 7.24). It is built to Le Corbusier's favourite dimensions 226×226 cm and presents a strange hermetic world of transparency causing the reader to pause and reflect. A trinity of Corbusian signs hover just proud of the glass of the cube to form a clue to the possible meaning of the space which they introduce – a fictive landscape of water and rock, bathed in the sun, drawn from Le Corbusier's distinct memories of his travels around and above South America. In an early photo in the *Œuvre Complète* the trinity consisted of two clouds and a sun (Fig. 7.25), but now the trinity is rather different, although its purpose, I would suggest, is similar. The first element, in natural wood, encompasses the door handle, its brown form evocative of a land mass when seen from above, or possibly a cloud (Fig. 7.26). The other two, flanking the side walls of the draught lobby, are emphatically clouds, but they are painted in a satin red (Fig. 7.15). Restrained by their metal fixings they do not touch the glass itself but are held proud of it as befits their floating state. The first red cloud is fastened to the glass with four fixings, the second with three – a further incidence of the number seven.

As though lifted from the pages of *Le Poème de l'angle droit*, the clouds and the land are familiar elements of Le Corbusier's symbolic language, but the sheer redness of the lobby clouds is startling. Red, in terms of *Le Poème de l'angle droit* is the colour of fusion, of carnality, of sex. It is about the body, the unconscious and basic instinct, qualities that Le Corbusier sweepingly ascribed to the Brazilian people, qualities that he delighted in when he visited their country.

In Le Corbusier's opinion "an architecture must be walked through and traversed… in the midst of a succession of architectural realities".[18] At the Maison du Brésil this "rule of movement" has been "brilliantly exploited". It is built around the viewer whilst utilising, and indeed flouting the rules of perspective. In this disorientating stage of the dramatic arc the visitor's horizontal, human viewpoint is temporarily held in suspense, replaced for an extraordinary and fleeting moment with a bird's eye view of clouds, land and sea – an entirely different "architectural reality" – as he or she moves through the lobby, where it is restored, upon opening the door into the hall itself, once more to the horizontal.

---

17   Fondation Le Corbusier (hereafter referred to as FLC) 12724 and 12725 in H. Allen Brookes (ed.), *The Le Corbusier Archive, Volume XXVIII* (New York: Garland, 1983), p.229. Hereafter referred to as Allen Brookes, *Archive*.

18   Le Corbusier, *Talks with Students* (New York: Orion, 1961), p.45. Originally published as *Entretien avec les étudiants des écoles d'architecture* (Paris: Denoel, 1943).

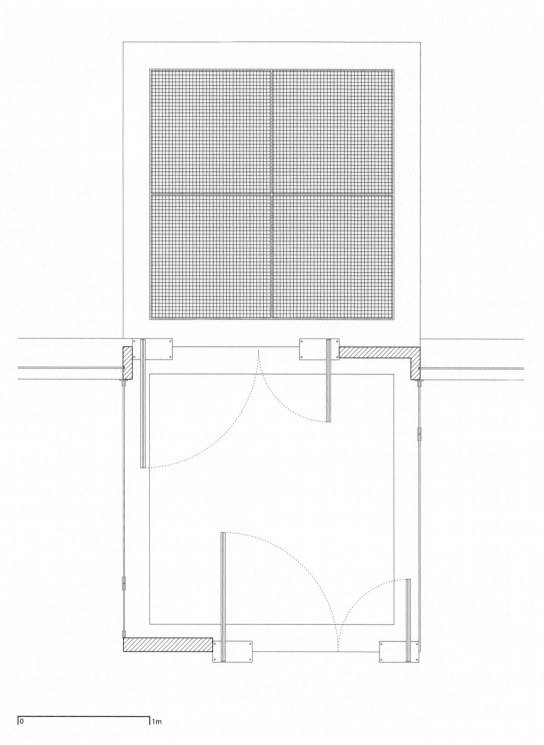

0 ⌐━━━━━━━━━━━━━━━⌐ 1m

7.21 **Plan of the entry vestibule of the Maison du Brésil (1957–59).**

7.22 **Entrance to the Maison du Brésil (1957–59).**

7.25 **Photograph of vestibule of the Maison du Brésil (1957–59) from the *Œuvre Complète*.**

7.26 **Handle of vestibule of the Maison du Brésil (1957–59).**

7.23 **Watery flooring in the Maison du Brésil (1957–59).**

7.24 **Glass vestibule at entrance to the Maison du Brésil (1957–59).**

...when one has gone up in a plane for observation and glided like a bird over all the bays, has turned around all the peaks, when one has entered the intimacy of the city, when one has torn away in a single glance of the gliding bird all the secrets that it hid so easily from the poor terrestrial on his two feet, one has seen everything, understood everything...

...when, by plane, everything has become clear, and you have learned this topography, this body so hilly and so complicated; when, having conquered difficulties, you have been seized with enthusiasm, you have felt ideas being born, you have entered into the body and the heart of the city, you have understood part of its destiny...

...But when everything is on holiday in Rio, when everything is so sublime and so magnificent, when one has taken a long flight over the city like a bird gliding, ideas attack you.[19]

Flight here is central to the pursuit of clarity that lies at the very heart of the promenade.

"The order of the day is intricate synthesis – bringing together viewpoints of an object from below and viewpoints from above", writes Le Corbusier's contemporary René Guilleré.[20] Le Corbusier took great delight in playing spatial games. "Try to look at the picture upside down or sideways. You will discover the game".[21] Vertical and horizontal – the right angle at the very heart of his personal philosophy – are blurred. Colin Rowe who devoted much energy attempting to chart the "perceptual intricacies" of Le Corbusier's work,[22] wrote of La Tourette, "for, if floors are horizontal walls, then, presumably, walls are vertical floors; and, while elevations become plans and the building a form of dice, then the complete aplomb with which Le Corbusier manages his church may, in some faint degree be explained".[23] The same could be said of the lobby of the Maison du Brésil. If, as Le Corbusier wrote, "the floor... is really a horizontal wall"[24] it follows that the wall is a glass floor giving a vertical view down through space. As Saint Exupéry wrote of the experience of a storm whilst flying:

Horizon? There was no longer a horizon. I was in the wings of a theatre cluttered up with bits of scenery. Vertical, oblique, horizontal, all of plane geometry was awhirl. A hundred transversal valleys were muddle in a jumble of perspectives... For a single second, in a waltzing landscape like this, the flyer had been unable to distinguish between vertical, mountainsides and horizontal planes.[25]

Passage through the vestibule brings about a metamorphosis – "bird flight, bird sight, extraordinary conquest. Harmonized destiny".[26]

Questioning – *savoir habiter*

In chapter 3 it was seen that Le Corbusier tried to make an architecture for Venice through reference to his experiences of the place. Something similar occurs in the Maison du Brésil where the third, questioning, stage of the dramatic narrative occurring here at ground floor level gives us a flashback to his own particular and pleasurable memories of Rio and of the sea there. "I swim in front of my hotel; I go back to my room by elevator in a bathrobe, at 30 metres above the sea; I stroll about on foot at night; I have friends at every

19   Le Corbusier, *Precisions*, p.235–236. See also "from a plane, one understands still many other things". Ibid., p.5.
20   René Guilleré quoted in "The Synchronisation of the Senses" in Sergei Eisenstein, *The Film Sense* (London: Faber and Faber, 1977), p.81. First published in 1943.
21   Le Corbusier, *The Chapel at Ronchamp* (London: Architectural Press, 1957), p.47.
22   Colin Rowe, *The Mathematics of the Ideal Villa* (Cambridge MA: MIT, 1976), p.192.
23   Ibid., p.197.
24   Le Corbusier, *Towards a New Architecture* (London: Architectural Press, 1982), p.172. Originally published as *Vers une Architecture* (Paris: Crès, 1923).
25   Antoine de Saint Exupéry, *Wind, Sand and Stars* (New York: Reynal and Hitchcock, 1941), p.83. Quote in Eisenstein, *The Film Sense*, p.83.
26   Le Corbusier, *Œuvre Complète Volume 4, 1938–1946* (Zurich: Les Editions d'Architecture, 1995), p.71. Originally published in 1946.

7.27 **View towards staircase in lobby of the Maison du Brésil (1957–59).**

7.28 **View towards the auditorium of the Maison du Brésil (1957–59).**

minute of the day, almost till sunrise; at seven in the morning, I am in the water".[27] This experience caused him to posit a vast town planning scheme where cars were to travel at roof level maximising contact with the sea in what he called a "seascraper" which would give vast bodies of people vital access to the beach.[28] The sensation of flight in the pursuit of clarity, of understanding, would be available every day for the inhabitant of the seascraper whose home would be "almost the nest of a gliding bird".[29]

Inside the building the vestibule interrupts the conversation between two staircases at diametrically opposing ends of the plan (Fig. 7.27). There are echoes here of the Maison La Roche, of the way in which Le Corbusier gave a certain presence to doors by making them burst through elastic space which pulls in the transverse direction. The staircase to the left of the main vestibule reads quite strongly in early plans of the lobby area but, in reality, does not impose its presence upon the space at all. It has none of the brazen attention seeking qualities of the stair in its neighbour the Swiss Pavilion, meaning that our focus is given to the travelogue of the ground floor barely distracted by the possibilities of a vertical route.

A low curved screen just ahead and to the right of the vestibule frames a gathering space beyond which the auditorium is accessed (Fig. 7.28). It is at this point that the centrifugal flow of the site described above meets an opposing force emanating from the auditorium, the result being a spatially charged vortex at the centre of the plan (Fig. 7.29) from which the reader spirals out in one of three directions, towards the auditorium, towards the offices, or up the stairs.

27   Le Corbusier, *Precisions*, p.234.
28   Ibid., p.239.
29   Ibid., p.244.

7.30 **Formwork of the ceiling of the lobby of the Maison du Brésil (1957–59)**
contributes to the centrifugal feeling of the space.

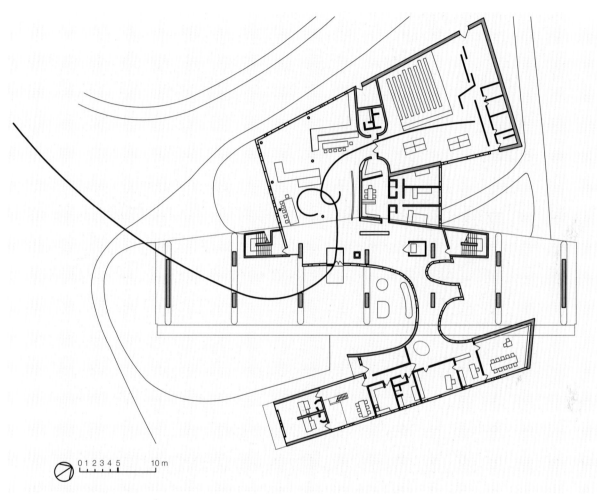

0 1 2 3 4 5   10 m

7.29 **Diagram showing spirals of movement into the heart of the lobby of the Maison du Brésil (1957–59).**

7.31 **Waiting space outside the Director's apartment of the Maison du Brésil (1957–59).**

The auditorium journey is given some status as it feeds directly off the vestibule. It is reinforced by the imprints of the planks of the concrete formwork in the ceiling which sweep and swell round in a dramatic curve (Fig. 7.30). At the same time there is a slope upwards in the floor from the vestibule towards the auditorium that distorts the perspective of the space and seems to accelerate its flow.

Objects in the landscape of the slate floor frame a series of implied spaces and thresholds through which the reader must pass, adding greatly to the richness of the experience of the ground floor. The door into the auditorium is aerodynamically crafted like an aeroplane's wing to minimise obstruction of movement, once more evoking the possibilities of flight. When closed, glazed panels around the door allow the sensation of space to continue unimpeded around it.

The area to the right of the vestibule slopes gently downwards indicating its lower order in the hierarchy of the space. It swoops round the curve of the forecourt wall to the director's apartment spiralling into a place for waiting, lit brightly by a lozenge-shaped rooflight (Fig. 7.31). A further tributary branches into the Director's apartment, where the onward thrust of the slate paving feels very strong in the narrow confines of the corridor. Just at the point where the corridor expands into the living room the slate is laid at right angles to the main route, halting the flow of space and giving a sense of calmness and arrival (Fig. 7.32).

7.32 **Corridor into living room of Director's apartment of the Maison du Brésil (1957–59).**

Reorientation

The narrative of land and water experienced from above permeates the landscape of the ground floor: a topography of rocks and water. Walking around at low altitude, slowly being indoctrinated into the delights of Le Corbusier's architecture, the reader cruises past the block of pigeonholes, a miniature Unité, cast not in concrete, but in glass (Fig. 7.33). This is the main point of orientation in the building. It occupies the charged zone between the two staircases. A block, a *casier* (storage box) indeed, not of apartments but of pigeonholes, it is formed of three bands. First a concrete foundation block that marks the ground plane. Onto this are mounted translucent pilotis sheltering the polished gray communal ground plane now occupied by a variety of potted plants and newspapers. Above these numbered glass cells provide individual homes for assorted letters and junk mail. The pigeonhole Unité is bolted together with metal plates like those of the lobby beyond, with which it is in conversation. This "jewel"[30] of the building, natural focus of the space, is lit from beneath like an altar, like the Unité itself, throwing a ripple of light onto the bulging concrete of the ceiling above, a reminder of something that never was. This is the zenith of the building around which movement ebbs and flows in frustrated perpetuity.

Summary

Higher up the building there is no single point of culmination, but multiple possibilities of release accessed through the individual cells. The vertical route through the building is played down in favour of another *implied* vertical route through the skies at lower level. Here the re-orientating qualities of the stair and the final stage of the promenade – culmination in the light above – are repressed, tucked away, superseded. The reader is left in limbo in the heaven of Rio as it should have been.

Jerzy Soltan recalled that for Le Corbusier the ground floor of a building "represented the poetic and purely visual longing to express the 'new space', the 'continuum of space', a relatively recent notion introduced by science and visually tackled already by Cubism".[31] What makes the Maison du Brésil so remarkable is that although it is fluid and open – you are free to walk anywhere – it comprises a carefully crafted route created out of the most minimal built gestures. The overlapping volumes noted in the promenade of Maison Jaoul B are at the Maison du Brésil so subtly expressed that they are almost imperceptible, but they are very much there in the experience of this building.

---

30   I owe this word to Denise Leitao who described it as "our jewel" when showing us around the space.
31   Soltan, "Working with Le Corbusier", in Allen Brookes, *Archive XVII*, p.xvi.

7.33 **Pigeonhole block in the lobby of the Maison du Brésil (1957–59).**

LA TOURETTE 1956–59

The Monastery of La Tourette is a reinterpretation of the rules of the Dominican Order established at the beginning of the thirteenth century. Penance through "regular observance" is central to the Dominican way of life, which requires the rigorous discipline of unruly desires for pleasure and comfort, and a concentration on the mission of the Order, spreading the word within a communal setting.[32] In chapter 3 I noted Elie Faure's belief that numbers played an important role in controlling the excesses of mankind. It is this taming of desire that, I argue, is absolutely key to the promenade of La Tourette. Giving some clues as to its underlying ambition Le Corbusier wrote that it "involves the presence of fundamentally human elements in the ritual as well as in the dimensioning of the spaces (rooms and circulation)".[33]

Le Corbusier included a plan of a traditional Dominican monastery in the *Œuvre Complète* (Fig. 7.34). He makes the point, slightly disingenuously, that it would be impossible to build a traditional cloister on a sloping site such as that at La Tourette. This is spurious as such cloisters have, in the past, been built in all manner of places.[34] The topographical issue is used as an excuse to separate out parts of the programme, creating points of tension in between them and in doing so producing a promenade much more evocative of what he saw as the contradictions and difficulties of monastic existence. At La Tourette there is a cloister, yet there is no cloister. Traditionally this paradisiacal garden is enclosed and protected by the ecclesiastical buildings within which it sits but, in this case, the cloister is left open allowing the rough hillside to come tumbling through the building, subverting any possibility of cloister implied by the form of the buildings above (Fig. 7.35). "The monastery is posed in the savage nature of the forest and grasslands which is independent of the architecture itself."[35] Le Corbusier talks in embattled terms of the position of the building within raw nature, as though it and the people within were desperately building barrages against it all.

The study rooms, work and recreation halls, as well as the library occupy the upper levels. Further down are layers of monk cells. Below this are the refectory and the cloister in the form of a cross leading to the Church. "And then come the piles carrying the four convent buildings rising from the slope of the terrain left in its original condition without terracing".[36] Some of the support structures bear an uncanny similarity to roots, meaning that the undercroft of the building feels like nothing so much as a tree partially torn up by its roots, again evoking nature at its least benign (Fig. 7.36).

---

32   www.curia.op.org/en/ accessed 17 June 2009.
33   Le Corbusier, *Œuvre Complète Volume 6*, p.42.
34   Indeed he originally admired the Acropolis for its use of plinths on an awkward site. Le Corbusier, *Towards a New Architecture*, p.43.
35   Le Corbusier, *Œuvre Complète Volume 7, 1957–1965* (Zurich: Les Editions d'Architecture, 1995), p.32. Originally published in 1965.
36   Le Corbusier, *Œuvre Complète Volume 6*, p.42.

7.35 **La Tourette (1956–59).**

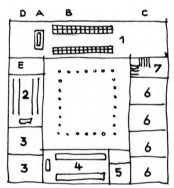

Plan traditionnel d'un couvent dominicain

7.34 **Diagram of a Dominican monastery from
the *Œuvre Complète*.**

7.36 **Rootlike foundations at La Tourette (1956–59).**

Threshold

Approaching along the leafy lane from the car park the blank wall of the Church, flanked by a much lower piano-shaped saddlebag of chapels, is the first part of the monastery to become visible in what Rowe describes as "some very private commentary upon Acropolitan material" (Fig. 7.37).[37] The Church itself has two sides and two entrances: one for the monks within, and one for the public without. As the reader rounds the corner of the Church, the angular thrust of the belfry comes into view. Here the fondness for anthropomorphism so evident at Ronchamp comes once more into play. Woman is evoked in the gable of the Church where she extends her cape over the gathered flock as in Piero della Francesca's *Madonna della Misericordia* (1462) (Fig. 7.38) or indeed the veiled woman that appears so frequently in his work, for example in the "labyrinth" section of *Le poème de l'angle droit* (Fig. 2.21), but she is left behind by the reader progressing steadily onwards. Le Corbusier, when at Mount Athos as a young man, dwelt on the impossibility of an existence without women – "thus everything is missing here in the East where only for the sight of her woman is the primordial ingredient".[38] The theme then in the approach to La Tourette seems to me to be the relinquishing of the body, of human love, in favour of a more spiritual union, the difficulties of which receive further expression in the design of the entrance.

An early model of the building shows a wall along the alley, on the East side of the building, blocking views of the internal cloister. This would mean that the reader would have to walk a good way without much to look at before arriving at the portal that marks the entry into the complex, in this way heightening expectation of what is to come (Fig. 7.39). Le Corbusier's buildings often went over budget – the source of funds for La Tourette being particularly restricted – the likely reason for the wall not being built to full height. Its absence makes the choreography of views en route into the building more chaotic than usual causing what Colin Rowe calls the lack of "preface" to the composition. If built as originally intended, the open portal would be set, like the doors in so many of Le Corbusier's buildings, within a taut horizontal band of wall protecting the space within. As it is, the composition does feel odd.

Sensitising Vestibule

The power of the open portal is reinforced by the contours of the land, meaning that it gives onto a space that is, in essence, a bridge spanning between two very different forms of existence (Fig. 7.40). In the floor a grating for the cleaning of shoes spans only half the width of the frame, as if waiting for a single file procession of monks. It is this – like so many of the spaces of monastic existence – both open to the air and under cover, that marks the vestibule of the building. The area protruding beyond the shade of the block is in essence a square, as is the space beneath it (Fig. 7.41), the pure form conferring a greater authority on the space than something more irregular. This vestibule space is occupied by a range of five extraordinary biomorphic pavilions that house the porter's lodge, the opulent curves of which are finished in a deep mottled gunnite plaster, similar to that of Ronchamp. Number five, as was mentioned in chapter 3, corresponds to the five senses. Lighting is brought into these bulbous forms through slots of red, which, as was seen in the previous

---

37   Colin Rowe, "La Tourette" in *The Mathematics of the Ideal Villa* (Cambridge MA: MIT, 1976), p.186.
38   Le Corbusier, *Journey to the East* (Cambridge MA: MIT, 1987), p.206. Originally published as *Le Voyage d'Orient* (Paris: Parenthèses, 1887).

7.37 **Side view of Church of La Tourette (1956–59) from the *Œuvre Complète*.**

7.38 **Piero della Francesca (1416–1492), *Madonna della Misericordia* (central detail), tempera on panel (c.1462). Pinacoteca Comunale, Sansepolcro, BEN-F-001167-0000.**

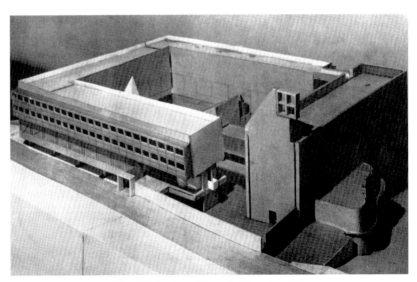

7.39 **Model of La Tourette (1956–59) showing wall from the *Œuvre Complète*.**

7.40 **Open portal that marks the point of entry into La Tourette (1956–59).**

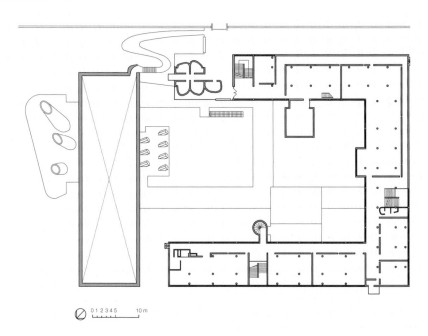

0 1 2 3 4 5   10 m

7.41 **Plan of La Tourette (1956–59) at entry level.**

7.42 **Seat at entry to La Tourette (1956–59).**

7.43 **Steep drop behind seat at entry to La Tourette (1956–59).**

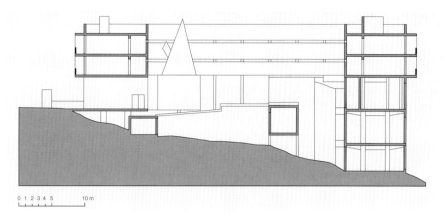

7.44 **Section across La Tourette (1956–59).**

case study, was for Le Corbusier the colour of the body and of fusion. The issue in the sensitising curves of the forecourt vestibule of La Tourette seems to be is the relinquishing of the sensual pleasure in favour of something more profound.

The reader is inflected from curve to curve along the axis of the bridge to a seat that hangs over the space of the cloister below (Fig. 7.42), the extreme use of what Geoffrey Baker calls "visual shock tactics" (Fig. 7.43). [39] Its presence invites the reader to pause and reflect upon the implications of entry, of rebirth, through the violent red door of the monastery. To sit in this seat is to turn your back upon the difficulties and dangers within the cloister, and to view the outer world once more (Fig. 7.44). At this point Rowe observes:

The visitor is so placed that he is without the means of making coherent his own experience. He is made the subject of diametric excitations; his consciousness is divided; and, being both deprived of and also offered an architectural support, in order to resolve his predicament, he is anxious, indeed obliged – and without choice – to enter the building. [40]

The door into the monastery is given significance by its overpowering redness, but there is little else in its detail to indicate its import. Indeed there can be few more anticlimactic moments in the glossary of Le Corbusier's architecture than arrival into what I will call the main stairwell of La Tourette (only because it appears near the main door – little else in terms of detail marks its superior position in the hierarchy of stairs). Generally there seems to be no particular justification for the positioning of the staircases which are not equidistant from one another. Nor do they line up with any other major events in the plan. In this way Le Corbusier subverts many of the usual tricks used by architects in the name of legibility, good space planning, economy and delight – tricks that he himself was all too familiar with.

Questioning – *savoir habiter*

There is no obvious pomp and ceremony in the architecture of La Tourette, just constant incitement to thought and reflection. The main circulation corridor at the level of the alley provides access to the oratory, the library and a variety of other communal rooms. It swerves curiously from the inner edge of the cloister to the outer perimeter and back again. The view of the inner courtyard is experienced and once more taken away. The justification for this is unclear.

39   Geoffrey Baker, *Le Corbusier: An Analysis of Form* (London: Taylor and Francis, 2001), p.307.
40   Colin Rowe, "La Tourette" in *The Mathematics of the Ideal Villa*, p.188.

7.45 **Circulation to the cells of La Tourette from the *Œuvre Complète*.**

7.46 **Window baffle at La Tourette from interior (1956–59).**

The circulation corridor at alley level, like that in the levels of monk's cells below (Fig. 7.45) finishes in a dead end where a window, presumably for air and light, is baffled (Fig. 7.46), preventing the view outwards and forcing the reader to retrace their steps (Fig. 7.47). At very least it seems as though Le Corbusier would have been interested in creating a spiralling route around the building – in some places a spiralling motion can just be perceived – but this is broken down just as soon as it starts to get into motion.

Within the main stairwell the finishes are rough and, as in much of the building, repulsive to the hand. Extremely low levels of artificial illumination produce a distinctly crepuscular atmosphere at night. Nicholas Fox Weber writes of the "challenging" nature of the stairs that link the levels of the building.[41] These long flights are of an unusually sharp incline. The spacing of the treads and risers is uncomfortable and physically demanding precisely because Le Corbusier wanted to bring focus back to the body as described in chapter 2. Further the centre wall of the dogleg is eroded at the lower level to make space for a vertical fluorescent light bulb resulting in an odd sensation that the stair is somehow supported on this flimsy column of light (Fig. 7.48).

The main stair feeds onto a corridor at base level (Fig. 7.49) which itself lines up with nothing in particular.[42] It cuts into the walkway that leads down to the Church, but it does not line up with the atrium as it could so very easily do. A further route leads on to the refectory, chapel and atrium, secondary to the corridor which slopes down to the Church which is framed in ondulatoire glazing devised by Iannis Xenakis and discussed in chapter 2 (Fig. 7.50). This gives a peculiar fluctuating rhythm to the experience of space as it expands downwards towards the entrance to the Church.

---

41   N.F. Weber, *Le Corbusier: A Life* (New York: Knopf, 2008), p.729.

42   There is a sub-route to the lower level of the Church at this point which is suppressed by various architectonic means meaning that the reader barely notices it.

7.48 **Low level light in stairway of La Tourette (1956–59).**

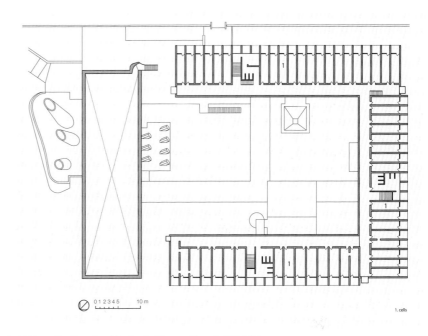

0 1 2 3 4 5   10 m

1. cells

7.47 **Plan of La Tourette at the level of the monk's cells (1956–59).**

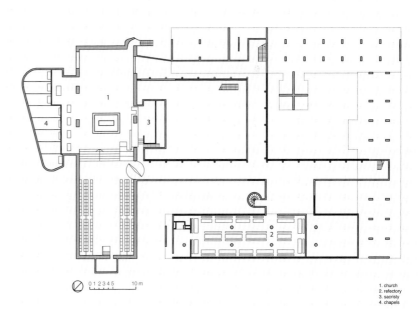

0 1 2 3 4 5   10 m

1. church
2. refectory
3. sacristy
4. chapels

7.49 **Plan at Church level of La Tourette (1956–59).**

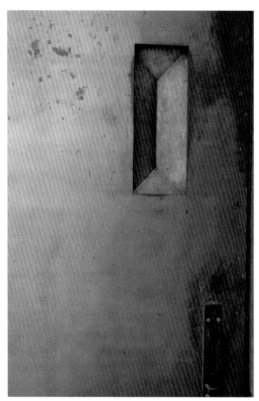

7.51 **Handle of the door to the Church of La Tourette (1956–59).**

7.52 **Handle of the door within the door to the Church of La Tourette (1956–59).**

The way is barred by a forbidding bronze door. It is facetted outwards like a jewel – its convex surface rebuffing entry. The riveted surface, tarnished with time, resembles nothing so much as the side of a tank or some other instrument of war. The handles of Le Corbusier's doors are generally a delight to touch, but not so in this case. Here a vertical slot frames a facetted back plate. To pull the door shut is to gain a precarious hold on the sharp rim of its opening. Abstract form and hard geometry afford nothing to the softness of the hand (Fig. 7.51). To open the vast bronze door at the end of the corridor would involve considerable physical effort. Even to open the little wicket gate within the door is difficult because of its extreme weight, and because of the high threshold that must be negotiated on entry (Fig. 7.52).

Once within, it becomes apparent that there is no dramatic conclusion to the vista. The corridor that leads down to the Church lines up with nothing within it other than the side of the steps leading up to the main altar (Fig. 7.53). This separates the territory of the monks from that of the main congregation who have their own access door from the main alley. There is a further altar at the monks' end of the Church which makes the priorities of the space yet more confusing. Added to this the extraordinary acoustic – a reverberation time of many, many seconds, sounds bouncing back from its deepest recesses – which stimulates questions in the mind about the extent of this uncanny space.

7.50 **Ondulatoires and door into the Church of La Tourette (1956–59).**

7.53 **View towards main altar of the Church of La Tourette (1956–59).**

As at the Maison du Brésil the floor is finished in Le Corbusier's *opus optimum*, meaning that the steps of the reader are continually mapped against the sequence of the Modulor. The traditional Dominican liturgy is characterised by its extensive use of bodily gestures: bowing, kneeling, prostrating, processing, all of which involve tactile engagement with the building where it takes place. When a Dominican monk prostrates himself on the Modulor floor of La Tourette its lines are imprinted on his body and he is absorbed into the radiant web of mathematical relationships that govern both the building and its environment.

Particularly intriguing is the dark void at the end of the monks' side of the Church (Fig. 7.54). Set into the wall, it is a geometric echo of the square in the ceiling above, which this time releases a blaze of light. It is almost as though projected from the dark square is the x-axis of the body set perpendicular to the y-axis of the spirit emanating from the hole in the roof above. All our movements are mapped within this grid. Le Corbusier wrote of Ronchamp that it involved the continual adjustment of a "thousand factors which in a true work, are all gathered and collected into a closely knit pattern – and even in the simple crossing of right angles, sign and symbol of an existence – these thousand factors about which no-one ought or would wish to speak of".[43] Here the right angle is implied within the architecture of the space. As Colin Rowe wrote of La Tourette, those "sceptical of the degree of contrivance" and "temperamentally predisposed to consider the game of hunt – the symbol as an overindulgence in literature" really need to look at the architecture once more.[44]

43   Le Corbusier, *The Chapel at Ronchamp*, p.6.
44   Colin Rowe, *The Mathematics of the Ideal Villa*, p.189.

7.54 **View towards the monk's side of the Church of La Tourette (1956–59).**

7.55 **Route to side chapel of the Church of La Tourette (1956–59) at high level.**

7.56 **The view down to the side chapels of the Church of La Tourette is suppressed by a yellow wall.**

There are three key light sources in the Church. The slot in the wall in the more public end of the building, the square hole in the ceiling at the other end, and the coloured circles set within the single-height space of the "piano", the exterior form of which is the first thing that the visitor sees on approach to the monastery up the alley. In order to reach this space it is necessary to step laboriously up and down over the corner of the main altar to its shelter (Fig. 7.55). This more intimate area is pleasantly lit by the rooflights that spill tantalisingly into the chapels below (Fig. 7.56). Yet, totally frustratingly, they appear to be completely inaccessible from within the Church itself.

It is necessary instead to go back through the Church, back out of the door and left through the hidden door into the sacristy to find a way down. From here a diminutive and highly compressed stairway leads through the bowels of the building into another chapel space and along a subterranean corridor to the piano-shaped side chapel. This bears an uncanny resemblance both in its form and in its relationship to the main Church, to the side chapel within the grotto at La Sainte Baume as it must have existed in Le Corbusier's time and still exists today (Fig. 7.57).

At La Tourette seven private altars are set within the piano-shaped saddlebag of space (Fig. 7.58). These are stacked in steps up the slope yet, contrary to what one might expect, there is no hierarchical climax to the space (Fig. 7.59). The topmost altars may be higher and wider but they receive no more light. The lowest altar is on its own giving it a certain importance but it is in a narrow gloomy corner. The top altar is coloured a

7.58 **Lowest level side chapels at La Tourette (1956–59) looking towards subterranean entrance corridor.**

7.57 Side chapel to the grotto of Mary Magdalene at La Sainte Baume.

7.59 Looking up the lowest level side chapels at La Tourette (1956–59).

7.60 **Rooflight in the side chapels at La Tourette (1956–59).**

bodily red while the bottom altar is a spiritual yellow, again contrary to expectations. Neither top nor bottom altar takes priority. In the dynamic equilibrium of this highly constrained space it is only the orbs of coloured light from the rooflights above that offer the possibility of release (Fig. 7.60). Here the final two stages of Le Corbusier's dramatic arc, reorientation and climax, are conspicuous by their very absence. All that is left is the ceaseless chant of generations of monks circling in timeless perpetuity, a seeming dead end, forcing the journey of the spirit ever inward.

Summary

"The composition of the convent starts at the summit and descends to the hollows of the valley in functional stages" writes Le Corbusier (Fig. 7.61).[45] It is traditional in architecture, including Le Corbusier's architecture, to progress upwards in pursuit of revelation. The opposite is the case in the early Christian catacombs in churches such as S. Clementi in Rome. Le Corbusier found within the roots of Christianity much in common with his own thinking on religion. Indeed the vertical journey excavated down into the most sacred parts of this building seems to echo Le Corbusier's own researches through the layers of Catholic doctrine to something altogether more pure. Given Le Corbusier's fondness for creating Jacob's ladders, connections between earth and sky, and his association of the vertical with the spiritual, it seems odd that the culmination of the route in the Church happens in relative darkness at almost the lowest possible level.

At La Tourette there are none of the easy movements and obvious clues that populate Le Corbusier's domestic work. Significantly his first instinct was to create, as was his wont, a dramatic denouement to the promenade up on the dazzling rooftop, but then he thought again, restricting access to the roof, in doing so negating its role in the overall journey. "I think you've all been on the roof and you've seen how beautiful it is. It is beautiful because you don't see it. You know, with me there will always be paradoxes… The pleasures of sky and clouds are perhaps too easy."[46] Instead Le Corbusier created sub-routes expressive of the inner turmoil and darkness (his Romantic roots emerge here with full force) of monastic existence.

La Tourette is, like *Le Poème de l'angle droit*, the product of two contradictory journeys. One is painful and complex leading down into the recesses of the earth, the other prohibited, a more enticing route up to the delights of the roofspace. Here, for Rowe, "an architectural dialectician, the greatest, was to service the requirements of the archsophisticates of dialectic", the Dominicans, hence the extraordinary tensions that are built into the programme.[47]

45   Le Corbusier, *Œuvre Complète Volume 7*, p.37.
46   J. Petit, *Un Couvent de Le Corbusier* (Paris, Les Editions de Minuit, 1961), p.28.
47   Colin Rowe, *The Mathematics of the Ideal Villa*, p.194.

Conclusion

In this chapter I have illustrated the ways in which the basic narrative structure of the promenade architecturale – exhibited most clearly in the Villa Savoye – could be manipulated or even truncated to fit in with the conceptual framework of these later more public schemes. This occurs most clearly at La Tourette where the promenade negates the usual narrative in an expression of the tortured life of a monk, and in the Maison du Brésil where the reader is left to absorb the watery and complex topography of the ground floor public space and Le Corbusier's regret at his inability to build there. In the Usine Duval the promenade upwards works in opposition to the factory process down through the building in an opposing traffic of material and spiritual contrast.

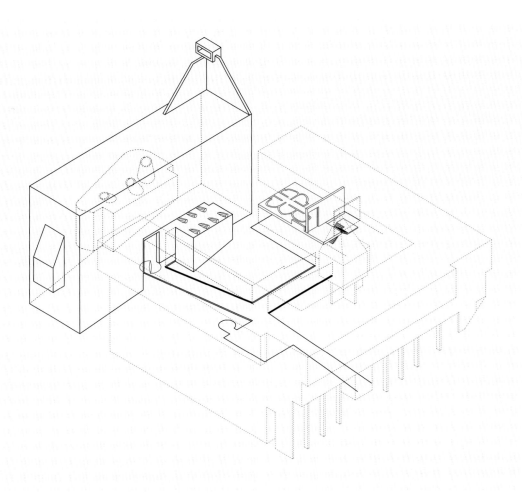

7.61 **Isometric of the elements of the promenade at La Tourette (1956–59).**

Initiation is absolutely central to Le Corbusier's architectural vision. Architecture then became the primary means of delivering his message of redemption, the promenade a built theogony designed specifically for the cause of conversion. Le Corbusier referred to himself, with characteristic immodesty, as the "architect of happiness". His architecture acts as a kind of *momento mori*, urging the reader to use his or her time on this earth well – *savoir habiter*. Creating an awareness of the passage of time seems to me to be essential to the creation of an environmentally and socially responsible architecture – it is one aspect of Le Corbusier's architecture that is redolent with possibility.

The elements of the promenade are never experienced in isolation, they always form part of a greater narrative. Each discrete element was designed to promote an engagement with the building and its meaning. A range of manipulative techniques were evolved to influence its course. The body plays a role of primary importance in this process, bringing about profound changes in behaviour and attitudes. At the same time careful framing of openings and the disposition of elements would resensitise the reader of the building to the possibilities of space and the intricacies of time. Lastly, by using what he called "a technique of grouping", Le Corbusier marshalled together objects and experiences into unified narratives designed to work upon the reader of the building at several different levels.

The exact nature of an experiential path through a building is difficult to pin down and to discuss, meaning that it is rarely given the attention that it deserves by architectural commentators. Yet other disciplines have risen to the challenge of evolving methodologies to understand sequences of sound and image in an intelligible way. Freytag's dramatic arc provides a useful medium for illustrating the ways in which the rules of rhetoric can be used to describe the build-up of a unified narrative, one that feels satisfying and complete, one that contains all the basic elements of a good story. This, with a slight adjustment of terms, can usefully be applied to Le Corbusier's architecture. A classic Jacob's ladder promenade type, such as the Villa Savoye, largely conforms to the five stages of Le Corbusier's narrative path – threshold, sensitising, questioning, reorientation and culmination. These stages have been used as a means to break down the promenade into its constituent elements, meaning that patterns can be seen, patterns that can then be creatively developed or usurped in other architectures. Whilst my method might be overly reductionist it reveals the way that the Jacob's ladder route is distorted and manipulated, particularly in the late work, to express a darker view of reality.

In Le Corbusier's early schemes his spatial games were somewhat laboured, the stages of the narrative arc more easy to identify. However, as he grew in both skill and knowledge, his architecture became vastly more subtle, less planar and more volumetric. It is the overlapping volumes of Le Corbusier's buildings that make his work so very compelling. Juhani Pallasmaa observes that "the quality of an architectural reality seems to depend fundamentally on the nature of peripheral vision, which enfolds the subject in space".[1] Further "the preconscious perceptual realm, which is experienced just outside the sphere of focused vision, seems to be just as important existentially as the focused image".[2] This is the precise point when the overlap takes hold.

It could be argued that the elements of the promenade are or should be the basic constituents of any building. All buildings should whet the appetite, have a functional core and an exciting culmination. In a sense it is the archetypal structure for all stories. It is this knowledge that makes the perverted route of La Tourette more disturbing. Towards the end of his life, deeply embittered by the frustrations of his architectural career Le Corbusier created the Venice Hospital, an extendable network of functional space, in many ways a commentary and reflection on all his previous work. Whilst a uniform cellular space like those of the wards of the Venice Hospital might appear to go against the hierarchy of the Jacob's ladder type, it too represents a form of initiation, this time into a depersonalised, disembodied, mathematical experience of nature as universal structure, the matrix of everything, as is only appropriate for an architect who was himself so intensely aware of his own impending death, the ultimate initiation, "the exit for each of us".[3]

Le Corbusier occupied a world that was intensely alive with energy and allusion, in which all things would come together in a state of unity.[4] His aim was to open the eyes of others to the possibilities of such a world using all the techniques that he had at his disposal to do so. This then was the purpose of the promenade, a metaphor for life's journey, finishing in ecstatic union with the cosmos. Yet while believing in such things he disbelieved, tortured by misgivings that his life work, his desire to create order, had in some sense been futile and pointless. It is in these moments of agonising doubt, expressed through the corrosion of the promenade, that his work gains its greatest force. This is the promenade taken to its more profound extremes. It is what you make of it that counts.

1   Juhani Pallasmaa, *Eyes of the Skin* (London: Wiley, 2005), p.13.
2   Ibid.
3   Pierre Joffroy, "Pourquoi le plus grand architecte fut-il le plus mal aimé?", *Paris Match*, September 11, 1965. Cited in N.F. Weber, *Le Corbusier: A Life* (New York: Knopf, 2008), p.20.
4   Flora Samuel, "Le Corbusier, Teilhard de Chardin and La Planétisation humaine: spiritual ideas at the heart of modernism", *French Cultural Studies*, 11, 2 (2000), pp.181–200.

Appendix

Selected Bibliography

Allen Brookes, H. (ed.), *The Le Corbusier Archive*, Volumes I–VII (New York: Garland, 1983).

Aristotle, *Poetics* (c.4bc), trans. Malcolm Heath (London: Penguin, 1996).

Arnold, D. and J. Sofaer, *Biographies and Space: Placing the Subject in Art and Architecture* (London: Routledge, 2008).

Baker, G., *Le Corbusier: An Analysis of Form* (London: Taylor and Francis, 2001).

Ballantyne, A., "Living the Romantic Landscape" in D. Arnold and J. Sofaer, *Biographies and Space: Placing the Subject in Art and Architecture* (London: Routledge, 2008).

Baltanás, J., *Walking through Le Corbusier: A Tour of his Masterworks* (London: Thames and Hudson, 2005).

Benton, T., "Villa Savoye and the Architects' Practice" in Allen Brookes, H. (ed.), *The Le Corbusier Archive, Volume* VII (New York: Garland, 1983), p.ix–xxii.

Benton, T. (ed.), *Le Corbusier: Architect of the Century* (London: Arts Council, 1987).

Benton, T., *The Villas of Le Corbusier 1920–1930* (London: Yale, 1987).

Benton, T., "The petite maison de weekend and the Parisian suburbs", in Mohsen Mostafavi (ed.), *Le Corbusier and the architecture of reinvention* (London: AA Publishing, 2003), pp.118–139.

Benton, T., *Le Corbusier conférencier* (Paris: Moniteur, 2007). Published in English as *The Rhetoric of Modernism: Le Corbusier as a Lecturer* (Basel, Boston, Berlin: Birkhäuser, 2009).

Benton, T., "Review Article: New Books on Le Corbusier", *The Journal of Design History*, 22, 3 (2009), pp.271–284.

Birksted, J.K., *Le Corbusier and the Occult* (Cambridge MA: MIT, 2009).

Branigan, E., *Narrative Comprehension and Film* (London: Routledge, 1992).

Breton, A., *Arcane 17* (Paris: Jean-Jacques Pauvert, 1971), p.66. Originally published in 1947.

Bruno, G., *Atlas of Emotion: Journeys in Art, Architecture and Film* (New York: Verso, 2007).

Bruno, G., *Public Intimacy: Architecture and the Visual Arts* (Cambridge MA: MIT, 2007).

Buchanan, S. (ed.), *The Portable Plato* (Harmondsworth: Penguin, 1997).

Burns, C.J. and Kahn, A., *Site Matters: Design Concepts, Histories and Strategies* (London: Routledge, 2005).

Carl, P., "Le Corbusier's Penthouse in Paris: 24 Rue Nungesser et Coli", *Daidalos*, 28 (1988), pp.65–75.

Carl, P., "The godless temple, organon of the infinite", *The Journal of Architecture*, 10, 1 (2005), pp.63–90.

Choisy., A., *Histoire de L'Architecture* (Paris: Edouard Rouveyre, 1899).

Cohen, J.L., *Le Corbusier and the Mystique of the USSR*, trans. Kenneth Hylton (Princeton: Princeton University Press, 1992).

Cohen, J.L., "Exhibitionist Revisionism: Exposing Architectural History", *The Journal of the Society of Architectural Historians*, 58, 3 (1999), pp.316–325.

Cohen, J.L., "Introduction" in Le Corbusier, *Towards an Architecture* (London: Frances Lincoln, 2007).

Coll, J., "Le Corbusier. Taureaux: An Analysis of the thinking process in the last series of Le Corbusier's Plastic work", *Art History*, 18, 4 (1995), pp.537–568.

Coll, J., "Structure and Play in Le Corbusier's Art Works", *AA Files*, 31 (1996), pp.3–15.

Colli, L.M., "Le Corbusier e il colore; I Claviers Salubra", *Storia dell'arte*, 43 (1981), pp.271–291.

Colli, L.M., "La couleur qui cache, la couleur qui signale: l'ordonnance et la crainte dans la poétique corbuséenne des couleurs" in *Le Corbusier et La Couleur* (Paris: Fondation Le Corbusier, 1992), pp.21–34.

Curtis, W., *Le Corbusier: Ideas and Forms* (Oxford: Phaidon, 1986).

De Smet, C., *Le Corbusier, Architect of Books* (Baden: Lars Müller, 2005).

Devoucoux du Buysson, P., *Le Guide du Pèlerin à la grotte de sainte Marie Madeleine* (La Sainte Baume: La Fraternité Sainte Marie Madeleine, 1998).

Dixon Hunt, J., *Gardens and the Picturesque* (Cambridge MA, MIT, 1992).

Duffy, E., *The Speed Handbook: Velocity, Pleasure, Modernism* (Duke University Press, 2009).

Eisenstein, S., *The Film Sense* (London: Faber and Faber, 1977). First published in 1943.

Eisenstein, S., Bois, Y.-A., Glenny, M., "Montage and Architecture" (c.1937), *Assemblage*, 10 (1989), pp.111–131.

Eliel, C.S. (ed.), *L'Esprit Nouveau, Purism in Paris*, *1918–1925* (Los Angeles: LACMA, 2001), p.25.

Emmons, P., "Intimate Circulations: Representing Flow in House and City", *AA Files*, 51 (2005), pp.48–57.

Evans, A.B., *Jean Cocteau and his films of Orphic Identity* (London: Associated University Press, 1977).

Faure, E., "La ville radieuse", *L'Architecture d'aujourd'hui*, 11 (1935), pp.1–2.

Faure, E., *Fonction du Cinéma: de la cinéplastique à son destin social* (Paris: Editions Gonthier, 1995). Originally published in 1953.

Forty, A., *Words and Buildings* (London: Thames and Hudson, 2000).

Freese, J.H., *Aristotle, The Art of Rhetoric* (London: Loeb Classic Library, 1926).

Gans, D., *The Le Corbusier Guide* (New York: Princeton Architectural Press, 2006).

Gere, C., *Art, Time and Technology* (Oxford: Berg, 2006).

Ghyka, M., *Nombre d'or: rites et rhythmes Pythagoriciens dans le development de la civilisation Occidental* (Paris: Gallimard, 1931).

Gothein, M.L., *A History of Garden Art, Volume 1* (London: Dent, 1928).

Grandidier, D., *Le Corbusier et St. Dié* (St Dié: Musée Municipal, 1987).

Gregory: D., *Geographical Imaginations* (London: Wiley, 1994).

Guthrie, W.K.C., *Orpheus and Greek Religion* (London: Methuen, 1935).

Heer, J. de, *Polychromy in the Purist Architecture of Le Corbusier* (Rotterdam: 010, 2009).

Hicken, A., *Apollinaire, Cubism and Orphism* (Aldershot: Ashgate, 2002).

Holm, L., *Brunelleschi, Lacan and Le Corbusier* (London: Routledge, 2009).

Hussey, C., *The Picturesque: Studies in a Point of View* (London and New York, 1929).

Ingersoll, R., *A Marriage of Contours* (New York: Princeton Architectural Press, 1990).

Jencks, C., *Le Corbusier and the Continual Revolution in Architecture* (New York: Monacelli Press, 2000).

Jenger, J., *Le Corbusier: Choix de Lettres* (Basel, Boston, Berlin: Birkhäuser, 2002).

Klonk, C., *Spaces of Experience: Art Gallery Interiors from 1800–2000* (London: Yale, 2009).

Krustrup, M., "Poème de l'Angle Droit", *Arkitekten*, 92 (1990), pp.422–432.

Krustrup, M., *Porte Email* (Copenhagen: Arkitektens Forlag, 1991).

Krustrup, M., "The Women of Algiers", *Skala*, 24/25 (1991), pp.36–41.

Krustrup, M., "Persona" in Krustrup, M. (ed.), *Le Corbusier, Painter and Architect* (Nordjyllands: Arkitekturtidsskrift, 1995).

Le Corbusier, *Towards a New Architecture* (London: Architectural Press, 1982). Originally published as *Vers une Architecture* (Paris: Crès, 1923).

Le Corbusier, *The City of Tomorrow* (London: Architectural Press, 1946). French edition: *Urbanisme* (Paris: Editions Arthaud, 1980). Originally published in 1925.

Le Corbusier, *The Decorative Art of Today* (London: Architectural Press, 1987). Originally published as *L'Art décoratif d'aujourd'hui* (Paris: Crès, 1925).

Le Corbusier, *Une Maison – un palais. A la recherche d'une unité architecturale* (Paris: Crès, 1928).

Le Corbusier, *Precisions on the Present State of Architecture and City Planning* (Cambridge MA: MIT, 1991). Originally published as *Précisions sur un état présent de l'architecture et de l'urbanisme* (Paris: Crès, 1930).

Le Corbusier and Jeanneret, P., *Œuvre Complète Volume 2, 1929–34* (Zurich: Les Editions d'Architecture, 1995). Originally published in 1935.

Le Corbusier, *The Radiant City* (London, Faber, 1967). Originally published as *La Ville Radieuse* (Paris: Editions de l'Architecture d'Aujourd'hui, 1935).

Le Corbusier and Jeanneret, P., *Œuvre Complète Volume 1, 1910–1929* (Zurich: Girsberger, 1943). Originally published in 1937, new edition: Zurich: Les Editions d'Architecture, 1995.

Le Corbusier, *When the Cathedrals were White: A Journey to the Country of the Timid People* (New York: Reynal and Hitchcock, 1947). Originally published as *Quand les cathédrales étaient blanches* (Paris: Plon, 1937).

Le Corbusier and Jeanneret, P., *Œuvre Complète Volume 3, 1934–38* (Zurich: Les Editions Girsberger, 1945). Originally published in 1938, new edition: Zurich: Les Editions d'Architecture, 1995.

Le Corbusier, *Talks with Students* (New York: Orion, 1961). Originally published as *Entretien avec les étudiants des écoles d'architecture* (Paris: Denoel, 1943), new edition: New York: Princeton Architectural Press, 2003.

Le Corbusier, *Œuvre Complète Volume 4, 1938–1946* (Zurich: Les Editions d'Architecture, 1995). Originally published in 1946.

Le Corbusier, *A New World of Space* (New York: Reynal Hitchcock, 1948).

Le Corbusier, "Le Théatre Spontané" in André Villiers (ed.), *Architecture et Dramaturgie* (Paris: Editions d'Aujourd'hui, 1980). Originally published in 1950.

Le Corbusier, *Poésie sur Alger* (Paris: Editions Connivances, 1989). Originally published in 1950.

Le Corbusier, *Modulor* (London: Faber, 1954). Originally published as *Le Modulor* (Paris: Editions d'Architecture d'Aujourd'hui, 1950).

Le Corbusier, *The Marseilles Block* (London: Harvill, 1953). Originally published as *L'Unité d'habitation de Marseille* (Mulhouse: Editions Le Point, 1950).

Le Corbusier, *Œuvre Complète Volume 5, 1946–1952* (Zurich: Les Editions d'Architecture, 1973). Originally published in 1953.

Le Corbusier, *Une Petite Maison* (Zurich: Les Editions d'Architecture, 1993). Originally published in 1954.

Le Corbusier, *Le Poème de l'angle droit* (Paris: Editions Connivance, 1989). Originally published in 1955.

Le Corbusier, *Modulor 2* (London: Faber, 1955). Originally published as *Le Modulor II* (Paris: Editions d'Architecture d'Aujourd'hui, 1955).

Le Corbusier, *Œuvre Complète Volume 6, 1952–1957* (Zurich: Les Editions d'Architecture, 1985). Originally published in 1957.

Le Corbusier, *The Chapel at Ronchamp* (London: Architectural Press, 1957).

Le Corbusier, *Le Poème Electronique* (Paris: Les Cahiers Forces Vives aux Editions de Minuit, 1958).

Le Corbusier, *Œuvre Complète Volume 7, 1957–1965* (Zurich: Les Editions d'Architecture, 1995). Originally published in 1965.

Le Corbusier, *Journey to the East* (Cambridge MA: MIT, 1987). Originally published as *Le Voyage d'Orient* (Paris: Parenthèses, 1887).

Le Corbusier, *The Final Testament of Père Corbu: a Translation and Interpretation of Mise au Point by Ivan Zaknic* (New Haven: Yale University Press, 1997). Originally published as *Mise au Point* (Paris: Editions Forces-Vives, 1966).

Le Corbusier, *The Nursery Schools* (New York: Orion, 1968).

Le Corbusier, *Sketchbooks Volume 1* (London: Thames and Hudson, 1981).

Le Corbusier, *Sketchbooks Volume 2* (London: Thames and Hudson, 1981).

Le Corbusier, *Sketchbooks Volume 3, 1954–1957* (Cambridge MA: MIT, 1982).

Le Corbusier, *Sketchbooks Volume 4, 1957–1964* (Cambridge MA: MIT, 1982).

Le Corbusier Plans, Echelle 1, Fondation Le Corbusier DVD, 2006.

Lee, P., *Chronophobia: On Time in the Art of the 1960s* (Cambridge MA: MIT, 2004).

Lowman, J., "Le Corbusier 1900–1925: The Years of Transition". Unpublished PhD thesis, University of London (1979).

Mâle, E., *The Gothic Image* (London: Fontana, 1961). Originally published as *L'Art Religieux du XIII° en France* (Paris: Armand Colin, 1910).

Mâle, E., *Religious Art in France: the Twelfth Century* (Princeton: Bollingen, 1973). Originally published as *L'Art religieux du XIIe siècle en France. Etude sur l'origine de l'iconographie du Moyen Age* (Paris: Armand Colin, 1922).

Maniaque, C., *Le Corbusier and the Maisons Jaoul* (New York: Princeton University Press, 2009). Originally published as *Le Corbusier et les Maisons Jaoul* (Paris: Picard, 2005).

McLeod, M., "Urbanism and Utopia: Le Corbusier from Regional Syndicalism to Vichy", PhD thesis, Princeton (1985).

Menin, S. and Samuel, F., *Nature and Space: Aalto and Le Corbusier* (London: Routledge, 2003).

Miller, F.P., Vendome, A.F., McBrewster, J., *Iannis Xenakis* (Mauritius: Alphascript, 2009).

Moles, A., *Histoire des Charpentiers* (Paris: Librairie Gründ, 1949).

Montalte, L. (E. Trouin pseud.), *Fallait-il Bâtir Le Mont-Saint-Michel?* (St Zachaire: Montalte, 1979).

Moore, R.A., "Alchemical and Mythical themes in the Poem of the Right angle 1947–65", *Oppositions* 19/20, (winter/spring 1980), pp.110–139.

Neumann, D., *Film Architecture* (London: Prestel Verlag, 1999).

Odgers, J., Samuel, F., Sharr, A., *Primitive: Original Matters in Architecture* (London: Routledge, 2007).

Ozenfant, A. and Jeanneret, C.E., "After Cubism" in Eliel, C.S. (ed.), *L'Esprit Nouveau: Purism in Paris* (New York: Harry N. Abrams, 2001).

Pallasmaa, J., *Eyes of the Skin* (London: Wiley, 2005).

Pearson, C.E.M., "Integrations of Art and Architecture in the Work of Le Corbusier. Theory and Practice from Ornamentalism to the 'Synthesis of the Major Arts'". PhD Thesis, Stanford University (1995).

Petit, J., *Un Couvent de Le Corbusier* (Paris: Les Editions de Minuit, 1961).

Petit, J., *Le Corbusier Lui-même* (Paris: Forces Vives, 1970).

Pico della Mirandola, G., *On the Dignity of Man* (Indianapolis: Hackett, 1998). Originally written in 1486.

Provensal, H., *L'Art de Demain* (Paris: Perrin, 1904).

Quetglas, J., *Le Corbusier, Pierre Jeanneret: Villa Savoye 'Les Heures Claires' 1928–1963* (Madrid: Rueda, 2004).

Rabelais, F., *Œuvres Complètes* (Paris: Gallimard, 1951).

Réau, L., *Iconographie de l'art Chrétien Volume 1* (Paris: Presses Universitaires de France, 1955).

Réau, L., *Iconographie de l'art Chrétien Volume 2* (Paris: Presses Universitaires de France, 1957).

Reiser, J., *Atlas of Novel Tectonics* (New York: Princeton Architectural Press, 2006).

Renan, E., *La Vie de Jesus* (Paris: Calmann-Levy, 1906).

Rodrigues dos Santos, C., Campos da Silva Pereira, M., Veriano da Silva Pereira, R., Caldeira da Silva, V., *Le Corbusier e o Brasil* (São Paulo: Projecto Editora, 1987).

Roller, T., *Les Catacombes de Rome. Histoire de l'art et des croyances religieuses pendant le premiers siècles du Christianisme, Volume II* (Paris: Morel, 1881).

Rowe, C., *The Mathematics of the Ideal Villa and Other Essays* (Cambridge MA: MIT, 1976).

Rowe, C., *The Architecture of Good Intentions* (London: Academy Editions, 1994).

Rüegg, A. (ed.), *Polychromie architecturale* (Basel, Boston, Berlin: Birkhäuser, 1997).

Rüegg, A. (ed.), *Le Corbusier Photographs by René Burri: Moments in the Life of a Great Architect* (Basel, Boston, Berlin: Birkhäuser, 1999).

Saint Palais, C., *Esclarmonde de Foix: Princesse Cathare* (Toulouse: Privat, 1956).

Samuel, F., "Le Corbusier, Women, Nature and Culture", *Issues in Art and Architecture* 5, 2 (1998), pp.4–20.

Samuel, F., "A Profane Annunciation. The Representation of Sexuality in the Architecture of Ronchamp", *Journal of Architectural Education*, 53, 2 (1999), pp.74–90.

Samuel, F., "Le Corbusier, Teilhard de Chardin and the Planetisation of Mankind", *Journal of Architecture*, 4 (1999), pp.149–165.

Samuel, F., "The Philosophical City of Rabelais and St Teresa; Le Corbusier and Edouard Trouin's scheme for St Baume", *Literature and Theology* 13, 2 (1999), pp.111–126.

Samuel, F. "The Representation of Mary in Le Corbusier's Chapel at Ronchamp", *Church History*, 68, 2 (1999), pp.398–417.

Samuel, F., "Le Corbusier, Teilhard de Chardin and La Planétisation humaine: spiritual ideas at the heart of modernism", *French Cultural Studies*, 11, 2 (2000), pp.181–200.

Samuel, F., "Le Corbusier, Rabelais and the Oracle of the Holy Bottle", *Word and Image: a Journal of verbal/visual enquiry*, 17, 4 (2001), pp.325–338.

Samuel, F., "La cité orphique de La Sainte Baume" in *Le Corbusier. Le symbolique, le sacré, la spiritualité* (Paris: Fondation Le Corbusier, Editions de la Villette, 2004), pp.121–138.

Samuel, F., *Le Corbusier: Architect and Feminist* (London: Wiley/Academy, 2004).

Samuel, F., "Animus, Anima and the Architecture of Le Corbusier", *Harvest*, 48, 2 (2003), pp.42–60.

Samuel, F., *Le Corbusier in Detail* (Oxford: Architectural Press, 2007).

Schumacher, T., "Deep Space Shallow Space", *Architectural Review*, vol. CLXXXI, no 1079 (1987), p.41.

Schuré, E., *Les Grands Initiés: Esquisse secrète des religions* (Paris: Perrin, 1908) in FLC.

Sekler, E. and Curtis, W., *Le Corbusier at Work: The Genesis of the Carpenter Centre for the Visual Arts* (Cambridge MA: MIT, 1978).

Soltan, J., "Working with Le Corbusier" in Allen Brookes, H. (ed.), *The Le Corbusier Archive, Volume XVII* (New York: Garland, 1983), pp.ix–xxiv.

Spate, V., *Orphism: the Evolution of Non-figurative Painting in Paris in 1910–14* (Oxford: Clarendon, 1979).

Stadler, L., "Turning Architecture Inside Out: Revolving Doors and Other Threshold Devices", *Journal of Design History*, 22, 1 (2009), pp.69–77.

Stirling, J., "Garches to Jaoul: Le Corbusier as Domestic Architect in 1927 and 1953" in Allen Brookes, H. (ed.), *The Le Corbusier Archive, Volume XX* (New York: Garland, 1983), pp.ix–xxi.

Teyssot, G., "A Topology of Thresholds", in Hebel, D. and Stollmann, J. (eds.) *Bathrooms Unplugged, Architecture and Intimacy* (Basel, Boston, Berlin: Birkhäuser, 2005).

Thomas, M. and Penz, F., *Architectures of Illusion: From Motion Pictures to Navigable Interactive Environments* (Bristol: Intellect, 2003).

Till, J., *Architecture Depends* (Cambridge MA: MIT, 2009).

Treib, M., *Space Calculated in Seconds* (Princeton: Princeton University Press, 1996).

Von Moos, S. and Rüegg, A. (eds.), *Le Corbusier Before Le Corbusier* (Yale: New Haven, 2002).

Weber, N. F., *Le Corbusier: A Life* (New York: Knopf, 2008).

Willmert, T., "The ancient fire the hearth of tradition: Creation and Combustion in Le Corbusier's studio residences", *arq*, 10, 1 (2006), pp.57–78.

Wogenscky, A., "The Unité d'Habitation at Marseille" in Allen Brookes, H. (ed.), *The Le Corbusier Archive, Volumes XVI* (New York: Garland, 1983), pp.ix–xvii.

Xenakis, I., "The Monastery of La Tourette" in Allen Brookes, H. (ed.), *The Le Corbusier Archive, Volume XXVIII* (New York: Garland, 1983), pp.ix–xiii.

Illustration Credits

The author and the publisher gratefully acknowledge the following for permission to reproduce material in this book. Whilst every effort has been made to contact copyright holders for their permission to reprint material in this book the publishers would be grateful to hear from any copyright holder who is not acknowledged here and will undertake to rectify any errors or omissions in future editions.

© F.L.C. / Adagp, Paris, 2010: all illustrations with the exception of:
3.11, 3.12, 4.5, 4.12, 4.14, 5.45, 5.5, 5.6, 5.14, 5.18, 5.21, 5.26, 5.28, 5.36, 5.37, 5.42, 5.44, 6.3, 6.7, 6.8, 6.17, 6.21, 6.24, 6.26, 6.27, 6.32, 6.35, 6.38, 6.41, 7.3, 7.4, 7.6, 7.7, 7.8, 7.10, 7.12, 7.14, 7.18, 7.21, 7.29, 7.31, 7.38, 7.41, 7.44, 7.47, 7.49, 7.61

© Flora Samuel:
0.1, 0.7, 0.8, 1.1, 1.4, 1.7, 2.1, 3.11, 3.12, 4.1, 4.3, 4.4, 4.6, 4.7, 4.9, 4.13, 4.14, 5.3, 5.7, 5.9, 5.10, 5.11, 5.12, 5.13, 5.14, 5.15, 5.16, 5.17, 5.19, 5.20, 5.23, 5.24, 5.25, 5.27, 5.28, 5.31, 5.32, 5.33, 5.34, 5.35, 5.37, 5.39, 5.41, 5.44, 6.1, 6.2, 6.3, 6.4, 6.5, 6.6, 6.9, 6.15, 6.16, 6.18, 6.19, 6.29, 6.30, 6.31, 6.33, 6.34, 6.36, 6.37, 6.39, 6.40, 7.15, 7.16, 7.17, 7.18, 7.19, 7.20, 7.21, 7.22, 7.23, 7.24, 7.26, 7.27, 7.28, 7.30, 7.31, 7.32, 7.33, 7.35, 7.36, 7.40, 7.42, 7.43, 7.44, 7.46, 7.48, 7.49, 7.50, 7.51, 7.52, 7.53, 7.54, 7.55, 7.56, 7.57, 7.58, 7.59, 7.60, 7.61

© René Burri, Magnum:
0.3, 3.9, 6.20, 6.22, 6.23

© Cabinet Ejzenstejn, Moscow:
0.4

© Alinari Archives, Florence:
4.5, 7.38

© Mauro Magliani for Alinari:
4.5

© Raphaelo Bencini for Alinari:
7.38

© Flora Samuel and Sam Austin:
4.12, 4.14, 6.17, 7.21, 7.29, 7.31

© Steve Coombs, Ed Wainwright and Flora Samuel:
5.5, 5.6, 5.9, 5.14, 5.18, 5.21, 5.24, 5.26, 5.28, 5.36, 5.37, 5.42, 5.44, 5.45, 6.3, 6.7, 6.8, 6.21, 6.24, 6.26, 6.27, 6.32, 6.35, 6.38, 6.41, 7.3, 7.4, 7.7, 7.8, 7.10, 7.12, 7.14, 7.18, 7.29, 7.41, 7.44, 7.47, 7.49, 7.61

© Stephen Kite:
7.1, 7.5, 7.6, 7.8, 7.9

© Bertrand Limbour:
7.2, 7.9, 7.13

Layout, Cover Design and Typography: Vera Pechel, Basel

A CIP catalogue record for this book is available
from the Library of Congress, Washington D.C., USA

Bibliographic information published by the German National Library
The German National Library lists this publication in the Deutsche Nationalbibliografie;
detailed bibliographic data are available on the Internet at http://dnb.d-nb.de.

© 2010 Birkhäuser GmbH
Basel
P.O. Box 133, CH–4010 Basel, Switzerland

Printed on acid-free paper produced from chlorine-free pulp. TCF ∞

Printed in Germany

ISBN: 978-3-0346-0607-3

9 8 7 6 5 4 3 2 1

www.birkhauser.ch